WIN THE
"WAR AGAINST LONELINESS"
ONCE AND FOR ALL!

Too good to be true? Not according to the thousands of single men and women—young, divorced, widowed, or simply disillusioned with their destructive dating patterns —who have already discovered that PAIRING works!

Dr. George R. Bach and Ronald M. Deutsch demonstrate the art of PAIRING through 54 clinical case histories, transcripts of actual encounter sessions between troubled couples, and tested, practical, easy-to-follow advice on making *authentic* contact with anyone, anywhere. You'll learn to unmask "Pairing Hustles"—the Stuffed Pairing, the Private Freedom Cult, the Con Man, the Isolation Ward, the Detective, and many others—and you'll discover how to enhance your own ability for sexual and emotional intimacy!

PAIRING

The revolu~~~~~~ ~~~~~ to beat

Other Avon Books by
Dr. George Bach

THE INTIMATE ENEMY

PAIRING

Dr. George R. Bach
and Ronald M. Deutsch

AVON
PUBLISHERS OF BARD, CAMELOT, DISCUS AND FLARE BOOKS

AVON BOOKS
A division of
The Hearst Corporation
1790 Broadway
New York, New York 10019

First Avon Printing: November 1971

AVON TRADEMARK REG. U.S. PAT. OFF. AND IN OTHER COUNTRIES,
MARCA REGISTRADA, HECHO EN U.S.A.

Printed in the U.S.A.

K-R   25   24   23   22   21

Contents

Society
versus the
single state
(an introduction)

THIS is a book about the hunger for intimate love and how it may be fulfilled. And so it is interesting to look for a moment at the culture in which that hunger is born and in which it is so consistently frustrated. For that culture is the most serious impediment to the very love it holds in such high esteem.

Ours is a family-oriented culture. And it so values family life that it treats unmarried adults at best as undeveloped, immature, and incomplete—and at worst as failures and willful renegades who cannot or will not take up a respectable and responsible family role. Even business succumbs to this prejudice, often automatically reducing credit ratings and raising insurance rates for single adults.

Singleness immediately raises questions about one's sense of responsibility and about one's desirability as a tenant, a neighbor, a customer, even a friend. The unattached man or woman, after all, may be cagily waiting for a chance to steal one's husband or wife.

Common stereotypes see the bachelor as a self-indul-gent hedonist, the unmarried woman as either pro-miscuous or frigid. With over nine million unmarried men and women in the most-marrying age group alone—from twenty to thirty-four—single adults con-stitute one of the largest and one of the most irration-ally discriminated against minorities in America. They are treated as second-class citizens.

It is only natural to want to escape from minority status to acceptability. And the pressure is added to by embarrassed families and concerned friends.

The insidious result is that—while giving lip serv-ice to the overriding importance of love—the vast majority of Americans actually make marriage status the real goal of male-female relationships. Pushed and cozened toward marriage, singles tend to test every contact with the opposite sex as a contact with a potential husband or wife. The chance for love disappears, we shall see, as men and women try to distort their perceptions of the other, of themselves, and of the relationship into good marriage bets. They dare not risk being authentic; it might spoil the sunny dream of rising out of tacit disgrace.

One consequence of this pattern of nonauthentic relationships is that only relatively few marriages incorporate intimacy; the rest are to some extent confining, unfulfilling associations with good poten-tial for divorce should serious crises emerge.

The pressure to conform to the cultural demand has another undesirable result as well. For many singles, each contact with the opposite sex is a threat. They become extremely cautious about state-ments or actions that might be construed as commit-ments. They fear being exploited as marriage part-ners. They keep their sexual relationships cool and distant (in the broad sense) and so deny themselves intimate rewards, for fear that genuine intimacy will force or entice them into marrying.

Still another consequence of this cultural orientation is a lack of scientific interest in what is plainly taken to be an undesirable state, and therefore a transitory one. The psychological literature on love contains an infinite variety of books and studies on marriage and the family, but precious few about the problems and welfare of the single adult.

The Institute of Group Psychotherapy in Beverly Hills, California, of which this book's senior author is founder and director, has always been interested in singles. But this interest intensified as seriously troubled marriages with little of value left, were referred to the Institute in a last desperate effort. When most such marriages inevitably broke, there was an obligation to try to deal with the psychological shock and distress of failure, of separation, and of re-entry into the single world. As these people were helped to avoid their previous errors of love and to establish genuine intimacy with new partners, it became apparent how early in a relationship intimacy was blocked and the seeds of failure sown.

As new techniques were developed at the Institute for eliciting intimacy and avoiding collusion, illusion, exploitation, and resentful accommodation, word of this work spread to other divorcees and to never-married singles who shared much of the same isolation and confusion. To serve these troubled men and women, their life styles, their wishes, and the reasons for their intimate success and failure were investigated. Techniques were then developed to counter the problems uncovered and to teach these methods in unique pairing clubs for adult singles. These clubs are special groups that are partly therapeutic and partly educational.

In our work with singles, we have come to deplore cultural strictures that condemn a mature choice of the single life, that ostracize the divorced man or woman as a failure, that treat the person who refuses to rush into marriage on greased skids of illusion as a misfit. But above all, we decry a culture that praises love in theory, but then—by demanding a primacy of marriage, and by supporting that primacy with a web of false custom, form, and expectation—denies the fulfillment of love to whole generations. That denial, we shall see, is bringing about a revolution against the old courting system.

G.R.B.
R.M.D.

1

The
intimate
revolution

BY the millions, men and women yearn for intimate love and cannot find it—not knowing how easily intimacy can be experienced, how effectively the emptiness can be filled.

Some are truly alone. And night after night, day after day, they stalk one another, at once both the hunters and the hunted. They prowl the singles bars and clubs and hotels and cruises and weekend trips. They haunt church socials and civic meetings, office water coolers and public tennis courts, the ski slopes and the beaches and the charter flights to Europe.

Robed and groomed and scented for the ritual, the brasher ones reach out, and the quiet ones watch and dream and wait. Then, with rare exceptions, everyone goes home, if not empty-handed at least empty-hearted, feeling a little more lonely, a little more hopeless—chilled in contrast with the warmth of communion they sought and did not find.

Others have lives that are filled, even over-crowded with people, or perhaps devoted to one important person they see regularly, sleep or live with. Yet most of them, too, have an inner sense of isolation. They feel a nagging, frustrated hunger for authentic intimacy that no amount of romance or infatuation, not even the engagement notice in the newspaper, may really satisfy. Why, they wonder, do they feel alone? Why does the old restlessness persist?

For both these groups the disappointment of the intimate longing is genuinely tragic. It leaves the disappointed empty, bitter, full of self-doubt. Some crowd the consulting rooms of psychotherapy. Most of them end by dismissing the longing as a naïve, adolescent dream. But it is adult, it is real, and it is necessary.

This yearning is well documented by the clinical research of the senior author of this book, in his work as consulting psychologist, with well over two thousand single men and women of all ages and from all walks of life. It is confirmed by his efforts with thousands more whose love had led to marriage but, as is the usual case, not intimacy.

It was from the understanding of these failures of love, and the solution of the resulting problems, that a system was evolved for overcoming fears and angers and false beliefs that barred genuine intimacy. During the last three years this system has been taught to numbers of men and women and has proven almost invariably, often startlingly, effective. We call the system Pairing.

Why does today's psychologist see intimate love as so important? Because what men and women seek from love today is no longer a romantic luxury; it is an essential of emotional survival. Less and less it is a hunt for the excitement of infatuation, or for the doubtful security of the marriage nest. More and more it is the hope of finding in intimate love something of personal validity, personal relevance, a confirmation of one's existence.

For in today's world, when men and women are made to feel as faceless as numbers on a list, they want intimate love to provide the feelings of worth and identity that preserve sanity and meaning. They hunger for one pair of eyes to give them true recognition and acceptance, for one heart that understands and can be understood. Only genuine intimacy satisfies these hungers.

When the quest for intimacy fails, personality is endangered. Those who fail tend to blame themselves, and to doubt their adequacy as men and women. They develop self-images of being cold, unfeeling, selfish, perhaps incapable of mature love and so doomed to inner isolation.

Since isolation is a prime cause of neurosis, they experience true neurotic symptoms—anxiety, anger, and depression. These feelings build the isolating walls still higher around them, shutting out the intimacy they seek, closing tightly the lonely ring.

Yet the walls and the ring can be broken. We have learned in clinical research that the great majority of men and women, contrary to their secret fears, are perfectly capable of the intimacy for which they long. They can quickly assimilate a new attitude, understanding, and style of loving. When they do, they learn how to see through the misguiding conventions and taboos, through the exploitation and anxiety that block them from genuinely intimate relationships.

In a surprisingly short time, they are able to *create* such relationships—rapidly, and with any of almost innumerable others. They can assess the potentials of such loves, realize them, sustain them, and if need be, end the associations with a minimum of pain for both partners.

In some respects, the purposes of the intimacy that is created vary as widely as the people from whose problems our pairing system came—people who were studied and counseled on college campuses and in youth groups, in work with divorce lawyers and conciliation courts, in group and individual psychotherapy with mature singles who felt isolated, in regular contacts with such divorce organizations as "Parents Without Partners." Their wishes ranged from companionship to better sexual expression, from loving friendship to eventual marriage.

On the other hand, some wishes are common to nearly all singles. Most want to meet new people and identify those with the best potential for true intimacy; to reduce their fears of rejection by others; to protect themselves from manipulation and exploitation; to guard against repeatedly choosing unrewarding partners. When they find a potential intimate, they want to get insight rapidly into what sort of partner he or she will make, and how to convey something of their genuine selves to him or her at once. In other words, they want to know how to make intimate love begin with a stranger.

When love does begin, they want to know how to make it grow, and how to keep one partner or the other from feeling either engulfed or held at too chilly a distance. They want to prevent being deceived by a well-meaning but over-accommodating partner, and to know how to compromise and cooperate without so smothering their own real wishes and feelings that they become inwardly resentful.

The pairing system provides some simple answers to these questions, all of which are based on the recognition and expression of authentic feelings. For we have no patience with the tactics, games, manipulations, and seductive tricks of either romantic tradition or of the current singles magazines. We know that they are as unhealthful and destructive to the manipulator as to the manipulated. They are barriers to intimacy. They alienate and isolate those who use them.

Indeed, the chief aim of the pairing system is to break down the illusions, in favor of authenticity, trust, and openness. To help people in therapeutic groups, such as our "pairing clubs," to do this, we lead them into real, intimate contacts with real partners, using special methods developed from therapeutic experience.

We hope that the reader will risk some of these experiences himself, by testing our methods—if single with a date, if married with his spouse. He can learn the methods from explanations in later chapters of this book. Each of them is designed to remove some important barrier to intimacy.

Certainly, enormous numbers of today's men and women, driven by their intimate longing, are impatient with the old non-intimate ways of loving—with the old etiquette, traditions, myths, and pseudoscience. They are experimenting with new styles and new ethics. A new and aware generation has sensed that the old ways—which we call the *courting system*—cheat them of intimacy. They are rebelling against that system and have begun an intimate revolution, to overthrow the romantic establishment.

The signs of the revolution are everywhere, as the rebels attack the institutions and forms of courting love. But despite their honest effort most of the rebels manage to cultivate only the outward semblances of the intimacy they seek. The closeness, the authenticity, the transparency, the freedom of expression of intimate love elude them.

Instead, they manage only an ersatz intimacy—with emphasis on public nudity, free-and-easy copulation, partner-swapping and an occasional orgy. Their "candor" is only a shadow—of four-letter words, self-pitying confessions, amateur psychoanalysis and encounter, and blunt attacks on others in the name of honesty.

When the sexes get together, the rebels end with only a shallow "togetherness" proximity. When they do away with stereotyped sex roles, they are left with the impotence and confused identity of "unisex."

The intimate revolution has so far produced only tantalizing glimpses of true intimate warmth, and the price has been high. Underneath, the old non-intimate system continues to operate. The roles and the rigid etiquette look changed, sometimes radically. But they function as before, masking reality and denying intimacy.

Plainly, though the intimate revolution has a bright banner and a powerful drive, it is doomed until it finds a method, and one that is not confining but free, self-expressive and genuine. Such a method, proven and workable, is *pairing*.

Some readers may be shocked by our concepts and methods, which disregard tradition. Even some professional colleagues are discomfited by our rejection of cherished beliefs and conventions of theory and practice.

But the fact is that the intimate revolution is under way. The old myths, rules, and philosophies are already under attack by those who are frustrated in their urgent push toward intimacy. The palace and the old laws are burning. We propose here a new, free, and realistic rule of love, one that we have seen bring fulfillment to those who long for it.

2

The pairing system

PAIRING is a new way of making love begin. To understand the system and how it leads to intimacy, it helps to understand the courting system—the old style and attitudes of loving with which today's adults have grown up.

Dictionaries define courting as seeking affection, trying to win applause or favor, holding out inducements. So when one courts, one puts on one's best face, inflates strengths, conceals weaknesses, and generally seeks to manipulate the other person. The courter neither presents the reality of his own self, nor explores the reality of his partner. The object is to create a sunshine smoothness without conflict, to capture by pleasing. Whatever might cause roughness or dissonance in the relationship is hidden behind illusions; it is avoided by as much giving-in (accommodation) as one can bear, and by the emotional tip-toeing required by "etiquette."

The courter begins by creating a façade that he thinks will attract. Having attracted a partner in this way, he may be saddled more or less permanently with the chore of playing the role that he has assigned to himself. He dares not step out of character for fear of perhaps losing some of his partner's love.

To be real, in the courting style of love, is to be endangered. And here trouble begins. For roles are by definition rigid. They become confining, stultifying. Beneath the sunshine surface, resentment grows.

Small wonder that courting partners are as much strangers when they love as when they meet, that they are likely to remain strangers in an affair or marriage. Small wonder that, for them, intimacy becomes impossible.

The divorced and more mature single people are especially dissatisfied with such surface love. They have traveled the road. They know it leads nowhere. Yet they cannot find an alternative. They are frustrated by what seems to them an inescapable trap of superficiality. They go through every intimate motion; they fall in love, they talk into the small hours, they live together. Yet intimacy seems to evade them. They are impatient with the time it takes to form and assess a relationship. They are bored and embittered by the secrecy that hides real feelings, by the adolescent maneuverings, the little seduction games, the good-time, fixed-smile dating routine.

Time and life, they feel, are wasting. And they sense that something is wrong at a deeper level. That something, traditional psychology holds, is probably neurosis. In the early history of the individual, something went wrong as the child developed his style of relating to others. In adulthood, then, some fear or anger blocks the fulfillment of the intimate longing. Most therapists believe that if the neurosis is resolved, intimate relationships are sure to form.

It is a reasonable sounding theory. In practice, it does not work well. Since failure to reach intimate love can cause neurosis, which came first, the neurosis or the failure of love? Also, if the traditional theory is correct, then perhaps ninety per cent or more of men and women are in need of psychological therapy. For only a handful of couples seem to achieve anything like intimate love. There are not enough therapists to listen even to a tiny fraction of these couples, and, besides, the therapy is not too successful. Popular impression to the contrary, when therapists, such as marriage counselors, hold meetings, one primary topic almost invariably is: why *is* their therapy effective in only a minority of cases?

The story of Jan, a divorcee who attended one of our pairing classes, illustrates the failure of traditional psychology in dealing with many intimate relationships. In her first session, she was asked why she had come to the class.

"I went right from a very sheltered school life into marriage," she said. "I never felt adequate for my husband in any way. I mean, I couldn't really talk to him about a lot of personal things, and I was frigid. After three years, we were divorced, and I went into analysis.

"After a year of that, I understood a lot about myself. I had been angry with men, and I wasn't any more. For example, I could come. I felt free, and I started having a lot of company and going to bed a lot."

"But why are you here?" one of the other girls asked. "You still haven't said."

"Because—" Jan answered, and her eyes were moist. "Because with all the men, I still feel alone. I can't really reach them. I'm not free. *I'm just an easy lay.*"

Neither Jan's freedom from old conventions, won by the intimate revolution, nor her inner freedom from the angers of her childhood, secured through psychoanalysis, had allowed her to create intimate bonding in love. The problem is an extremely common one.

The ideal of the courting system might be expressed as the formula: *one plus one equals one.* Two people are to become one flesh, one heart, a new entity known as "We," and the individuals supposedly recede or disappear. The proposition is as difficult emotionally as it is in mathematics. It means that each partner's answer to any important question ought to match the other partner's. Many experiences have been reported in our pairing classes to show the hamstringing absurdity of this idea.

Julie is asking Nick, a fellow college student, about a test-yourself quiz she is reading in a magazine:

JULIE:
Do we like to use four-letter words during sex?

NICK:
(Looks up warily, uncertain about what to say.) Well, we have used them sometimes, I guess. I mean, what kind of four-letter words?

JULIE:
Well, I suppose words like—(she becomes uneasy and watches him.) Like for—doing things, and body parts, I guess. I don't know. Do you think we like to?

NICK:
(He does sometimes like to be blunt. But he is being

asked what "we" like, so he maneuvers to please.)
You've used them sometimes, haven't you?

JULIE:
Yes. But I think only after you do.

NICK:
Hmm.

Such "we" conversations become fencing matches,
testing grounds for courting roles. Nick and Julie
hesitate to commit themselves, for fear of what the
other will think, so both become cautious and self-
conscious about using any coarse language during
intercourse. Each thinks that the other one thinks
such language is indelicate. In point of fact, both
are turned on by explicit words during sex. But their
courting style has now cut them off from a small but
mutually satisfying expression.

Today's intimate revolutionaries usually ignore the
"we" concept. Unable to reach intimacy, they often
try to convince themselves that they do not want
any interdependence. Their cult is autonomy—
independence carried to the extreme.

"You do your thing," their philosophy goes, "and
I'll do mine. No questions or promises. If by some
lucky coincidence we happen to get together now
and then, groovy. Beautiful." It is not really beautiful. It is lonely. It is as fruitful as insisting that *one
plus one equals one plus one*. One is not changed by
the other.

Traditional psychology often produces a similar
effect by counseling: "One cannot really make another happy or unhappy, and one cannot take responsibility for another's emotions. So one simply plays out
one's own hand. The partner does not have to stay if
he does not want to. He is responsible for what

happens to him. One must work out conflicts within oneself and then learn to accept whatever results in one's relationships."

We often compare this to the building of a fire. Conventional psychology sees two logs; the better the logs, the better the fire. So it aims to perfect the logs, on the assumption that the fire will take care of itself.

We have found this approach to have limited effectiveness. Our philosophy and understanding of intimate relationships may be expressed by the formula: *one plus one equals three*. The three elements are: the man, the woman, and their relationship.

To us, the crucial element is the fire between the logs, the dynamics between the pair. While our students might take years to understand themselves, they can be taught to see and understand their relationships very quickly. And when they are mobilized toward good relationships, the buried fears and angers within the individual tend to be resolved. Psychoanalysis proves to be unnecessary for most of those who can achieve intimate love by pairing. And most can.

Obviously the old courting system persists because it serves some real emotional needs. What are they? Studying courting behavior, we were struck by the endless role-playing, the complex web of illusions that the partners spun, the careful collusions with which the partners maintained these illusions. Plainly, the role-playing and illusions of courting hide the reality of the individuals and their relationship. When reality is denied, it is because it is frightening. So the courting system must persist because it deals with some important fear.

What fear? We found that courting illusions had much the same theme: "We are *right* for each other, so we automatically please and fulfill one another. Real conflict must be kept hidden at any price because it would signify that we are not predestined lovers, after all."

So the fear from which the courting system protects people is a deep and powerful one, the fear of rejection, of separation from love. Except for fear about survival, there is probably no more potent emotion in the human heart.

Rejection fears appear very early in any relationship. As soon as affections are engaged, the courting lover begins to feel a subtle tension and discomfort. Poets call these feelings lovesickness and, ironically, often celebrate them as *proof* of love.

The lovesick partner feels something like this: "I am tense and uneasy, because I am trying hard to guess what you want me to be, so that you will love me. Once I psych out what you find lovable, I will bend myself out of shape to conform to your idea of lovability for fear you may stop loving me. I dare not show you my real self, because I feel inadequate, since I know inwardly that I do not exactly fit your notion of lovability. And I am afraid to take a real look at you, too, because you might not fit into my idea of what is lovable."

This feeling is destructive. It is usually perceived only as a vaguely weakened identity and sense of worth, as a kind of wistful loneliness. Underneath, usually hidden even from himself, the lover is resentful and feels trapped because he cannot express what he authentically is.

The pairing system deals with the same fears, not by concealing them, but by confronting and resolving them. Once these fears are dealt with, the bars to intimate love are down. If one can handle the fears, one need not hide from them or from the realities that produce them. If one can then be genuine, so, usually, can one's partner. For genuineness creates trust and confidence.

The pairing partner has no need to manipulate and exploit to get what he wants of another. He can ask, without guilt, and what he gets is given freely, without prices or strings. Pairing also helps with sex problems because those that are emotionally caused result from hidden fear or hostility.

When a woman withholds her orgasm, or when a man ejaculates prematurely, for example, hostility is often the reason. Such partners are saying to one another: "I will not allow you the fulfillment of feeling like a complete man or woman."

Since pairing permits and demands open expression and resolution of fear and anger, these emotions need not be expressed covertly, in or out of bed. Pairing also eliminates the common fears that to love is to submit to control and become engulfed. These fears often mar sex by blocking a surrender to the experience. Pairing reduces these fears by reinforcing the sense of worth and identity.

When intimate love is created by pairing, the lover feels: "I am more myself because I know that you see me as myself. I know that the authentic me is the person you love. So I can be that person fully and proudly and with delight."

Love expressed through pairing, intimate love, never causes lovesickness. It brings a sense of joy and well-being. The pairer does not feel static, but free to change and grow. His horizons become enlarged by love, not narrowed.

An old adage of love is that men and women ought not to try to change one another. The courter, of course, does not dare to change; he would produce deep anxiety in himself and his partner.

The pairer can respond to reasonable, specific requests for change in his behavior. He can take the risk because he feels loved in reality, and so his risk is small.

This book is written in the hope—and with clinical evidence to make the hope realistic—that the reader who longs for genuine love can be guided toward it by an understanding of intimacy. Marriage is not the object. The authors' interest is in the forming and maintenance of intimate relationships between men and women. Marriage is only an institution in which such relationships exist. In itself, it provides only familiarity, not intimacy. In fact, because marriage always requires certain kinds of role-playing (boss, mother, breadwinner) it often makes intimate love all the more difficult to achieve.

Sociologists agree that the institutions of love are changing, and that many may die or be converted to new forms. We make no attempt to predict what will happen. But we believe that, whatever the forms and institutions, the essential problems of intimate love can be solved only through relationships that are open, acute, and authentic.

3

Making
pairing
contact

THE would-be pairer, moving about in a world of
three billion people, is tantalized by hundreds and
thousands of potential partners who seem always to
be just out of reach. It seems sometimes as though
these partners all wear little signs over their hearts,
saying: "DO NOT APPROACH. VIOLATORS
WILL BE HUMILIATED AND REJECTED." The
proscription is worst of all for a woman, who, because
of cultural taboos, still feels that she damns herself if
she reaches out.

So single men and women turn to friends or rela-
tives or therapists or newspapers advice columns or
single magazines and ask, "Where can I meet people—not the nothing people I see at the meetings I
go to, sitting and saying trivial things, not the
swingers who spout superficialities at the bars and
weekend spots, not the no-depth athletes—but real
people?"

Ironically, the questioner is frequently in the
presence of some of the people he is looking for. But
they are wearing masks to suit the occasion.

Chances are that he, too, is wearing his mask and a mind filter that blocks all but the most superficial impressions of other people.

For the people he sees are trying to fit in, to match. They present themselves in a ritualistic way. They try to behave appropriately according to the setting in which they appear. On the beach they flex their muscles. At meetings they concentrate on the problems of the business at hand. On the dance floor they concern themselves with dance style. Under the masks, one may be sure, are interesting and lonely faces. But the intimacy-hunter is busy preserving his own façade in order to hide his fear of being rejected. He is afraid to expose his genuine self and too self-concerned to elicit reality from others. So he and his peers become accommodating mirrors for one another, *things* for mutual convenience—to make a quorum, fill out a foursome, dance with, display beauty and power for, or warm a double bed.

We have an absurdly easy answer for the singles who ask us where to look for intimacy. It is, "Wherever you are."

This may sound flip, but what we are really saying is that the "where" is not very important, when one seeks new opportunities for intimacy. What matters is the spirit, the "how" of seeking. In our pairing programs, we have found that, once our concepts of the intimate eye and the open, genuinely eager, questing heart are well understood, the "where" question is answered almost automatically. And the old courting restraints fall away.

The courting ethic has left many painful ironies in its wake. But none is sadder than the commonplace of lonely people who feel gagged, unable to cry out, and bound by invisible ropes from moving toward one another.

Appalling absurdities mark the courting manner of initiating intimate contacts. One of them is the tradition of the permissible accident.

For months, Ken and Peg have seen each other in the office-building elevator. Never for long, because each looks away as soon as the other enters. But in timorous glances out of the corners of their eyes, they have seen what they liked. Lately, they have risked small smiles of recognition, but nothing more.

Ken would like to speak. But he is afraid that she might laugh. She might even get furious. ("Officer! That man has exposed his feelings to me in a public elevator!")

She feels much the same. He might scoff. ("Run along little girl.") He might be disgusted. ("What is this, Miss? A sexual solicitation to speak to you? That's promiscuity!")

So they remain silent, insular. It is only decent. It is only safe. Then the elevator stops—suddenly. They are alone.

PEG (anxiously):
What's wrong?

KEN (puzzled):
It seems to have stopped. I mean, there must be a power failure or something.

PEG (after a pause of 45 seconds):
We won't fall?

KEN:
Oh, no. These things are fail-safe. I've already pushed the alarm button three times.

PEG:
I wonder how long before I'd have thought of that.

KEN:
You must work for Thresher and Black.

PEG (nods):
You must be with Balladay and Company. I've noticed where you always get on.

KEN:
You noticed? (She blushes. He smiles.) You always carry legal papers, big stacks. I always want to help.

PEG:
I'll let you from now on. (Smiles.)

KEN (He takes a deep breath):
I've noticed some things, too. You wear those soft sweaters. They make you look so fragile.

PEG:
I'm stronger than I look. You should see my tennis serve. It's a cannonball.

KEN:
I'd think your long hair would have got in the way before you cut it last month. I liked it.

PEG:
You cut yours, too. I was glad. Those sideburns weren't you. You look nicer Ivy League.

KEN:
My girl liked it long.

PEG (crestfallen):
Oh.

KEN:
Maybe that's why I cut it as soon as we broke up.

PEG (relieved):
Oh—Well, I don't have anyone to tell me how to wear my hair.

KEN:
Are you accepting applications?

PEG (daringly):
Only from people who take me to lunch.

KEN:
I'm on my way to lunch now—and—We're moving!

The isolation is broken, but against great odds. For the courting culture looks to a chance proximity for human contact. It is not "proper" to break one's shell deliberately. One must wait for Fortune to drop the egg. So one waits eagerly. Who will be in the next seat on the airplane? Who goes to the same church, joins the same club, has the same mutual friends, rents the apartment next door?

Chance proximity removes neither the threat of rejection nor the threat of dubious intent. The man in the next seat at church could be an axe murderer. And rejection remains a menace always.

One who tries to make contact may be rejected as unattractive or unworthy. He or she has also lost bargaining strength. Defenses come tumbling down when people perceive the message, "I am interested in you." Whoever gives such a signal confers great power upon the person to whom he makes it.

There can also be danger in being accepted. Perhaps the "interested" other will prove to have a bad disposition or bad teeth. Then one would suffer the embarrassment of having to end by rejecting him. Similarly, people tend to be cautious about the contact attempts of others, feeling that one small assent may lead to a chain of unwanted pressure.

The point is that anxiety is often great enough to inhibit the wish to get together. Yet accident tips the balance in favor of approach. Here is how some pairs make contact:

"Both our names began with A, so we sat next to one another in high school for three years."

"I was alone on the trail, three miles from camp, when I fell, and if Henry hadn't come along . . ."

"I went off the high board, and my top broke, and there beneath me was Irv, and . . ."

Outside our pairing classes, people listen to such stories and wait for their turn to meet a potential intimate by accident. They wait for someone to enter the safe circle of love, what we call the *pairing village*.

The size of that village grows radpily in the young years. Love is first perceived as an almost automatic warmth from the presence, the sounds, and the breast of mother. Mother always loves Baby, automatically. So, one learns in a few months, does Daddy. And gradually one expects love from all that may be titled Family.

This kind of love is extended immediately, on demand. It is part of the instant gratification of infancy. When Baby wants the breast, he wants it NOW. He has no patience with any intermediate steps that precede feeding. Adults understand that first the coin must be earned, then the food bought and prepared and served. Gratification is somewhat deferred.

But Baby does not want to wait. He is shocked, when he begins to have playmates, to learn that love has a *quid pro quo*, a price, and it may not come instantly.

He quickly understands, however, that he belongs to villages, circles, where automatic acceptance is probable. He finds it among the kids on the block, or in school. He is cautious of strangers. Maybe they will be rejecting.

Adults take a similar position. And the problem with this position is, it turns potential intimates into symbols——such as co-workers, fellow members, classmates, and so on. One looks for symbolic green lights, rather than people, and in curious, needlessly far-fetched ways.

Sam and Betty often see one another on the city bus in Chicago, but naturally, they never speak. Then one morning Sam sees that Betty is reading her hometown paper. He lights up.

SAM:
Excuse me. You couldn't be from Duston, Texas?

BETTY (a little suspiciously):
I might be.

SAM:
I went to General Houston Grammar School and Alamo High.

BETTY:
I don't believe it! I went to Kit Carson!

SAM:
Want me to hum the Kit Carson fight song?

Contact. Yet here is a curious paradox. Duston is a town of thirty-seven thousand people. Had they both been on the same bus in Duston every morning, they would probably still be strangers.

The illusion of safety of the village can and should be extended almost infinitely. Suppose Sam and

Betty had come from opposite ends of the nation. Now they hear one another's accents as they shop as tourists on a remote Greek Island. Under these circumstances they still accept one another as fellow villagers. Only now their village is all America and their potential intimates number over two hundred million!

It is easy to see the absurdity of such conventions. Yet it is hard for many people to change their attitudes. They want a symbol, like a safe-approach pass, to allay their fears.

Eavesdrop on girls at the sidelines of a dance. "Yes," you hear, "I'm dying to meet him. But what can I do? Walk right up and say, 'Hello, I'm me?' "

Our response is: why not?

Before people can present themselves with such openness (and without feeling foolish or afraid), they need not only develop an intimate eye and a questing heart. They must also learn the art of impacting, ways to meet rejection without fear, and other techniques. But along the road to these methods we must first clear away more of the underbrush left by the courting system.

4

The myth
of matching:
Computer, computer
on the wall

NEVER before has a generation been so free of
practical impediments to intimacy. Why are they
still cheated of genuine love? What shibboleths remain to cheat them?

Consider Paul, twenty-six, and Susan, twenty-
four, a brave new pair, born of our brave new
world. Science and philosophy have long yearned to
see such a couple joined without many of the old
fears and ignorances. It has taken centuries of search
and struggle and change to make them as they are.

They are tall and straight and bright-eyed, living
testimonials to the good diets, the early immuniza-
tions, and the antibiotics of our new medical era.
They are free of most of the physical scars of the old
childhood diseases and the deprivations.

They feel little real insecurity about poverty for
themselves. They have heard of the Depression, but
it never really touched them. They tend to take
almost as birthrights the good clothes they wear, the

warm houses they live in, the quiet, automatic cars they drive.

Psychological science helped in their upbringing. Both of their parents read Spock and Gesell, and so became aware of how children develop. So the pair are not burdened by serious hang-ups from such errors as impatient toilet training, clumsy weaning from the breast, or the disapproval of infant sex play.

Advanced education freed them from much that is superstitious and opened their minds. They have considerable tolerance; it permits them to communicate across many old walls of separation—walls of religion, politics, class, and even color.

Education has also endowed them with unprecedented self-awareness. Paul and Susan accept thoughts and actions that once were sources of needless shame. As youngsters, they could masturbate with little fear or guilt. And today they can look back calmly on meaningless homosexual incidents during pubescence. They do not mind discussing sexual feelings toward parents and siblings. And they are informed about emotions in themselves and others—the hostility that can lie within laughter, the hidden wish that creates accident, the language slip that reveals a suppressed meaning.

They rebelled as well as they could in adolescence. But there was really little to rebel against, so permissive was their upbringing. Their parents exercised little control after puberty. To rebel in a satisfying way, in fact, they had to reach outside the family—to find rigidity where it still existed in such authority figures as the draft board and the college administration.

As adults, they have free choice of which clothes they wear, what work they do, where they live, or whom to marry. Paul and Susan choose to live in a singles apartment complex outside Los Angeles and recently met there. They live independently, yet have wide access to other singles at the tennis court, the swimming pool, and the Saturday-night dances staged by the recreation committee. No one cares whether they end up in his apartment or in hers for breakfast Sunday morning. Naturally, they feel free to discuss such things in the local encounter group that they both attend on Wednesday evenings.

They have dated twice in the last two weeks. And they are now returning from the neighborhood theater, where they have just seen a Swedish movie featuring poetic but forthright depictions of both ordinary and Lesbian intercourse.

As they converse, the first holdover from the old courting system emerges. It is the device we call *imaging*. We borrow the word, appropriately, from public relations, the world of the image makers. It refers to the attempt to create a favorable impression in the mind of one's partner, by dramatizing traits one thinks will be deemed attractive.

Susan, observing Paul's longish hair and hip dress, has assumed that he favors things in the new free style, and will approve of liberated speech and action. She does not know that his background and emotional style are quite similar to her own. She is not aware of this because Paul is also imaging. He is picking up the themes she sets, since he wants to appear to have similar tastes. For this reason, for example, they both often drift a little uncomfortably into four-letter speech rescued from Anglo-Saxon farming and Victorian shock. They use it, of course, in casual settings and in the cool manner.

PAUL:

Well, I can't see what everybody thought was so shocking about that one. It's a very sensitive film.

SUSAN:

It was really very poetic. I thought the fucking scene was really neat, didn't you?

PAUL:

One of the best I've seen lately. But you know, it did seem to me they went on awfully long with the cunnilingus bit. I mean, just because you show it in public, what's so sensational? People are still so ridiculous about sex.

SUSAN:

Right on. I mean, you wouldn't think anyone would have to go to a movie just to turn on, would you?

PAUL:

I can't really see why. If it's sex they want, wouldn't you think they'd just go and do it?

SUSAN:

There must still be a lot of square people around. Did you read how shocked a lot of people got about that Danish porno exhibition—just because they had a fucking demonstration? I mean, what kind of a demonstration would you expect in a sex exhibit?

PAUL:

Sure. What *would* you expect?

SUSAN:

Imagine if they did anything more interesting—like a demonstration with two men, instead. It would probably blow everybody's minds.

PAUL:

Why would that be more interesting to you?

SUSAN (covering her concern that she may somehow have said something "wrong"):
Well—that doesn't shock *you*, does it? It's interesting because I haven't ever seen it, that's why. You were watching those two women in the movie tonight, weren't you?

PAUL:
That's true. Anyway, it doesn't shock me. After all, nothing natural can be shocking, can it?

SUSAN:
That's just what I was thinking! You know, we really seem to think a lot alike.

PAUL:
We do, don't we?

Here the imaging is edging toward attitudes that both feel to be of basic importance in a relationship. It is a ritual that both have conducted since their first meeting. They continually compare and try to match their tastes, styles and values. It is amusing. But it is also a matter of earnest. For it is to this matching that most pairs turn to learn how "suited" they are.

Almost any preference is meat for matching. For our culture believes firmly—and this is taught in the "Family Living" and "Mental Hygiene" courses—that this is how men and women can make realistic judgments about the potential of their relationships. Paul and Susan are now making themselves comfortable in Susan's apartment.

PAUL:
Say, this is neat. (He looks around.) And I like that van Gogh print. He's one of my favorite artists.

SUSAN:
Is he? Mine, too. I don't know just what it is, the color and vitality, I guess.

PAUL:
Yes, that's what it is.

SUSAN (she starts to put records on her stereo):
What do you like, Paul? The Association, the Beatles—

PAUL:
Either one. (The music begins.) Why, I have that *same* album! (He beams with the discovery.)

SUSAN:
Really? Mine is almost worn out. The first two bands, anyway. They really turn me on. I think it's the freaky lyrics that make me flip.

PAUL:
Right on. It's the first two bands that made me buy the album.

SUSAN:
Really? (She smiles broadly.) I'm afraid all I have to drink is vodka. (She looks to him for a reaction.)

PAUL:
Oh, that's cool.

SUSAN:
I—(She hesitates, uncertain whether to risk a confession.) I'm not much of a boozer.

PAUL (he watches her, then smiles):
Well, it's really all I like to drink. Because you can't taste it so much. I never liked the taste of whiskey.

SUSAN (looks at him fondly):
Me neither. You know, I really—(She hesitates

again, then decides on the risk.) I really sort of wish I liked pot. But it just makes me cough and feel dizzy.

PAUL:
You too? (He looks delighted.) I tried it with hash a couple of times, but it made me nervous.

SUSAN:
Nervous?

PAUL:
Well, to tell the truth, I keep thinking all the time, what if I get busted? Maybe it's the square in me. I mean, sure I went to school at Berkeley, like I said, but I did grow up in Canton, Ohio.

SUSAN (beams again):
Well, Lincoln, Nebraska, is not exactly where it's at. But that was a lot too square for me. Wow. I just always felt out of it, you know, different from the other kids.

PAUL (nods understandingly):
Back in Canton, I used to think there was something wrong with me. Now I figure it really wasn't me; it was them.

SUSAN (with a wide grin):
Right on.

Added to the previous matching information, the score looks better and better to Susan and Paul. There are parallels in social class, education, religion, money, taste, style, and future aspirations.

To both, the constantly appearing bits of likeness seem amazing. Neither stops to consider that van Gogh pleases almost everyone. They do not think that there are millions of Presbyterians, middle-class middle-Westerners, and even more Beatles fans.

Some of their matching is a crude attempt to use psychology. Note, for example, their delight in having shared the adolescent experience of feeling different from other youngsters back home, an almost universal phenomenon among small-town people who move to large cities.

Now and then they do strike a difference. And their handling of it is worth noting. On one occasion their conversation turns to children.

SUSAN:

Well, I just don't think I want any. You know, with all the overpopulation and that. Why, I read, in India—

PAUL:

No children at all?

SUSAN:

Well, do you think intelligent people should?

PAUL:

Who else should? I know I'd want a couple of kids.

SUSAN:

Oh? Well, I saw what it did to my mother, how dependent it made her, how—helpless, and I don't know ...

PAUL:

The right man wouldn't let that happen. I know I'd want my wife to go on doing things outside the house. Women can have families and still do a lot in the world nowadays.

SUSAN:

You feel that way? (Edgily.) Of course, partly it

was that my mother married too young and started having babies right away. I guess a woman could wait to have children until she was thirty, maybe even older.

PAUL:
Sure. A couple ought to have some years to have fun by themselves, after all. That gives the man a chance to get on his feet financially, too. And I agree with you on the overpopulation bit. Start having kids too young and you may wind up with too many. I mean, even one child would really be enough.

SUSAN:
I guess it really is an experience any woman would want to have. After all, one child, when she was in her thirties and she'd had time to do things—

This basic conflict, which suggests possible deep problems for the future, is simply smoothed over. Paul and Susan handle all conflicts similarly. They smooth them and then change the subject as quickly as possible. They are really "illuding" themselves, convincing themselves of a false perception of reality, building an illusion into an apparent fact and future source of misunderstandings or worse. The real fact remains, for example, that Susan is very reluctant about childbearing, and that Paul is certain he wants to be a father.

Before leaving her apartment that night, Susan had followed the advice she had read in a national magazine aimed at single women. She had left her bedroom door open, with the light on and the bed turned down, a signal of willingness.

Not that Susan is promiscuous. She makes love only when she genuinely feels affection and has had some chance to know her partner. So she has never regretted sex or felt demeaned by it.

She and Paul are becoming close, and it is more sensible to find out if there are any sexual hang-ups before they get deeply involved. Anyway, why deprive themselves? It has been several weeks since Susan has had sex, and she would not want to associate this frustration with Paul. Besides, she reasons, what better way to get to know someone than by going to bed? The Pill handles any remaining fear.

In the following weeks, the physical intimacy increases the intensity of their relationship and, with it, the energy of their matching effort. They look everywhere for similarities, even—with a self-conscious air of amusement—in horoscopes, palms, tea leaves and Tarot cards. Even in bed they pretend that each likes what the other likes. No serious difference is permitted to appear that cannot be smoothed over, as was the question about having babies.

Eventually, the balance of decision is tipped. The two lovers experience what many still consider the ultimate omen of modern love. They have a simultaneous orgasm! The die is cast. Soon the wedding date is set.

A little more than a year later, they file for divorce. They are bewildered and disenchanted. They believed that they had taken every reasonable precaution. Though both are hurt, they try to be civilized about it. And they usually succeed, except for an inability to remain in the same room for half an hour without sniping or screaming at one another.

What, sociologists ask, could destroy so well-matched, so carefully prepared a pair, in so Utopian a time for pairing? Even after marriage, they appeared to enjoy every freedom. For example, when their sex life all but ceased after six months of marriage, both were able to tolerate outside dating by the other spouse, and even to discuss the experiences. What threat, what inhibition had they suffered that made them angry and drove them apart?

Some of their friends decided that their basic error had been marriage itself. The friends maintained that the restrictive feelings aroused by a formalized relationship were enough to do the damage. They said that Paul and Susan should simply have lived together, until they decided that they wanted to have children.

What had happened here, even Paul and Susan realized, was a failure, not of marriage, but of the basic human relationship. Yet, since marriage is the only sexual institution for which records are kept, it is the only source of statistics for the frequency of pairing failures.

They are common indeed. Since 1955, the number of divorced people in America has more than doubled. And there are, in addition, almost as many separations. One divorce decree is being handed down for each two marriage licenses issued, and the relative frequency of divorce is increasing rapidly. All authorities agree that even these high figures would be overwhelmingly larger if countless pairings were not held together by children, religion, feelings of obligation, guilt, fear of being alone, or lack of money.

The sociologists say new institutions are going to have to be invented to replace marriage and the family as they are now constituted. Many are suggesting legal trial marriages, after which a permanent certificate might be issued. Others point out that so many couples are now living together without any legal agreement that legalities may be superfluous. Margaret Mead, Virginia Satir, and other social scientists are advocating pairing contracts of two to five years duration. These could be canceled or renewed at expiration. A somewhat more radical wing believes there ought to be an end to marriage of any kind, and proposes various kinds of insurance programs to provide security for children.

Psychotherapists know that the situation is just as troublesome outside marriage. After a year together, even Paul and Susan were aware that their battles over sex, money, children—almost everything except van Gogh—would have been just as bitter without the wedding rings. Dating and courtship cycles are breaking and reforming faster and faster. Decisions to mate, in whatever form, are less and less frequently based on the psychological realities.

An army of observers seeks to explain the great modern pairing failure. They blame everything from the wars to pills, from pot to dirty movies, from the scattering of families geographically to the no-bra look, from Communism to free sex, from unisex to Women's Liberation. Each group of partisans threatens and censors and teaches according to its own lights. But the trend does not change.

Neither does the belief in matching. And so social scientists pour rules and statistics into their textbooks, ignoring the personal dynamics that are the real determinants of the potential for intimate love. They see the potential in static terms, much as they might try to fit pieces into a jigsaw puzzle.

Which attributes, they ask, are most significant for happiness? Then they arbitrarily define happiness in terms of high or low divorce rates for various matchings. The state of Iowa, for example, has done much analysis on the effects of religious differences on divorce. In a typical instance, Iowa finds that when a Catholic marries a Lutheran, rather than another Catholic, the divorce risk rises by some six per cent. Such small differences hardly explain why so many pairings fail.

Characteristically, many scientists have felt that if this questionable raw data were put into computers, along with the characteristics of masses of would-be lovers, the ultimate in matching would be achieved. This idea has proven to have commercial value. One sends the computer people a check and the answers to such questions as:

"How much do you earn?"

"Is sex important to you?"

"Should a wife be faithful to her husband?"

"Do you object to the drinking of alcoholic beverages?"

"To what political party do you belong?"

Plainly, such matching is going to have dubious value. For one thing, many of the questions would produce much the same answers from millions. Almost everybody is interested in sex, accepts social drinking, and enjoys the theater. The "votes" for such items are much too large to be meaningful.

But even if reasonably meaningful determinants can be arrived at, the authors have been unable to find any scientific evidence that matching likes and dislikes makes for good pairing. We decided to test how effective computer programs could be.

The purpose of this original research project was to compare adult male-female partner choices for intimacy potential between objective (statistical-computer) selections and subjective personal selection. A further research aim was to track changes in potential intimates during a long hotel weekend devoted to personal growth.

The experiment was conducted twice, with two different groups of singles. The second set of results, validated the original study, which went like this:

Twenty-four adult single males, aged twenty through fifty-one—half never married and half with one divorce—met twenty-four adult single females, aged twenty through forty-four—half never married and half divorced once. None of the forty-eight participants had previously seen any of the opposite-sex members, although some of the males knew each other and so did some of the women.

After they all practiced the communications exercises of the Pairing System, Charles and Mel, the two men voted by the computer program as least likely to succeed, finished the weekend with the greatest number of choices as potential intimates by the women.

Curt, for whom the computer picked six strong matches, was in reality rejected by five of them; only one woman, Frances, liked Curt as much as the computer program thought she would. However, Curt did not agree with the computer. He preferred Libby, even though she was not among the six potential intimates picked for him by the computer.

On the basis of a personal meeting, Libby rated Curt as "pretty good." However, Libby's very first choice (she rated him "WOW") was Rudy, whom the computer failed to consider even as a possibility for Libby. Instead, Rudy was computer-matched with three other ladies, none of whom gave him the WOW rating. And so it went.

The computer program missed other selections. In their personal-contact choices, the men tended to concentrate on and compete for the five physically most attractive women, while the women did not develop such body worship. The females spread their interests in a broader choice pattern, reducing the competitive element that males apparently enjoy.

The computer selections not only missed this trend; they predicted the reverse. The computer would have had the ladies concentrate on four males: Curt, Bernie, Jim, and Van. Among the ladies the computer selections failed to come up with any superstars.

In the beginning, the females were more involved. They were very conscientious and warmed up quickly to the communication exercises. The males tended to be reserved, even skeptical. They held back, casing the situation, before they would really join the girls. Both sexes were anxious, even fearful about what was to come in this unusual program. Yet the females, with as much or more inner fear than the males, showed courage (or trust) sooner than the males.

However, as the weekend progressed the males more than caught up. As a group, they were in the end more deeply touched by the obvious development of genuine intimacy. The fact that Friday strangers had become Sunday afternoon close friends, seemed to impress them considerably more than it did the females, who felt more natural about the experience.

At the end, the females knew better how to part, how to say good-bye cheerfully. They had had fun, a meaningful encounter, and a good group-learning experience. They were satisfied and ready to return to their regular city life pattern. Many more males showed signs of separation-anxiety. They were in no hurry to leave. They definitely wanted more. Once their appetite for intimacy had been whetted, they felt acute hunger for it and regretted having held back in the beginning.

The Institute now conducts training retreats for singles three to four times a year and these sex differences have shown up again and again. So we devised ways of helping males to speed up their warm-up process during the beginning sessions of the weekend retreats. They respond well to this, which shows that most psychologically significant sex differences are not inborn and therefore can be reshaped by social and therapeutic learning.

Computer matching must fail for many reasons. First, the statistical-mathematical probabilities of good "scientific" matching are extremely low because the complexity of the process involves an almost infinite number of variables. Furthermore, human nature dicates that the partners' standards for making their choices vary and contradict each other. Should the computer be programmed on the basis of similarity or contrast? Or on the theory that opposites really do attract, or that they will misunderstand or bug each other? Are sociological, status, occupational, and religious factors very relevant, slightly relevant, or largely irrelevant to intimacy potential? Since none of these questions can be answered by any program, all computer matching programs function without sound scientific basis.

Second, the programming depends on rigid questionnaire answers checked by computer customers. The answers are assumed to reflect stable states or traits of personality, attitude, value, or taste. The assumption that any person has a quasi-permanent structure is rarely warranted. The only reliable personality data comes from the psychotics who cannot help but be "reliable" because of the involuntary rigidity caused by their illness.

Normal, healthy adults are very fluid, or potentially so, especially more fluid when they are interested in developing an intimate relationship. *The personalities of a pair of intimates during the relevant phases of deep mutual involvement are actually characteristic of that one pair only.*

For example, the qualities that Curt draws out of Libby are dramatically different from the self-descriptive matter that Libby checks off on a cold questionnaire. Curt is not dealing with a Libby-in-general, but with a Curt-involved-Libby, who is quite a different lady. A scientifically oriented psychologist would not try to predict the result of a fluid, emerging, *inter*-personal dynamic event from individual personality data. The results can only be produced by the experience of the budding relationship. It simply does not exist beforehand and, therefore, the questionnaire data are ironically irrelevant to predicting intimacy potentials.

Computer matching schemes are really social introduction services dressed up in pseudoscience to reduce embarrassment. But their machinery contains the seeds of failure by robbing strangers of initial contact-tension and rejection fears. So "introductions" of any kind have a lower chance for launching true intimacy than do-it-yourself efforts to reach out everywhere: the laundromat, the office, the subway, the market, the movies, the coeducational programs for adults at university extension evening schools, and the weekend retreats, conducted by workshops and seminars on psychology and the art of living conducted by the one hundred or more therapeutic growth centers that have sprung up following the pioneering model of Esalen in Big Sur, California.

Even some of those who are selling computer services have grave doubts about the value of their matching. One of the first venturers in the field finally advised customers to stop looking for the perfect match and to accept the idea that the computer only provided them with a larger pool from which to choose partners. The same entrepreneur complained, incidentally, that his service tended to draw "the perfectionist, the supercritical, the intolerant, and the inflexible." And a New York sociologist who set up a matching-by-computer enterprise commented that many people who bought his service had "fantastic" dreams that could not be fulfilled.

Customer dissatisfaction is widespread in this industry. And some authorities have questioned many of the operations. When the Los Angeles District Attorney's office filed suit against one computer service, one of its investigators said: "We didn't publicize it because we didn't want to hurt the legitimate services. But as time goes on, the less legitimate they seem." And California's chief Deputy Attorney General, Charles A. O'Brien, commented: "Fraud in this field preys on people's loneliness and invades their privacy to an unusual degree . . . The complaints we have been receiving recently indicate that we must take a close look at this industry."

Such industrial fraud, no matter how lamentable, is not really our major concern. We worry about the intimate frauds that well-meaning men and women perpetrate upon themselves and others as they seek to pair.

Our real concern is whether the idea of matching holds real meaning for lovers. We conclude it has little, if any. We suspect, for example, that some computer customers use the machines as replacements for parents. The object would be twofold—to revolt against real parents, and at the same time to disassociate oneself from the responsibility for pairing decisions. It is a displacement of authority by electronics.

Matching is mostly a breeding ground for illuding. Any two lovers who wish to "feel matched" rationalize their illusion simply by denying or smoothing over any items for which matching does not work.

If matching is no realiable basis for pairing, what is left? What about love feelings? How real and meaningful is love's intuitive electricity, and how realiable? How close does love bring lovers toward intimacy?

5

The all-electric meeting: How love and fear begin

EVERYONE has quite different memories of love, but much the same dream of how it begins. And now and then the dream becomes real; it happens.

They are strangers when they arrive at the party. Then suddenly, they find themselves in the same corner at the same time—at the bar or the buffet. They exchange a few casual, ordinary words. But for some reason, their speech is nerve-strung and hesitant. Their laughter comes a little too quickly, a little too easily, with perhaps a note of hysteria.

In a curiously short time, they are saying very open, intimate things in a very direct way. Many of these things have to do with the sensual—with taste or touch, with aroma or appetite. All the while, their eyes keep flicking into little bursts of contact, like charged wires brushing in the wind.

An outsider who chances to overhear their conversation may get little idea of what is happpening between the two. But if he *watches* the couple, he can learn much more, for the outward signs of fire are visible.

He sees the flush in their cheeks, the moistening of their intent eyes. He observes the tensions in the postures of the head, neck, and body—the man's chest perhaps swelling slightly, the woman's hips tending forward. He notes the tight unsureness of their hands, which spill just a little of a drink, or drop an unlighted cigarette.

The couple, for in a very few minutes they have become a couple, are keenly aware of a growing physical warmth between them. They feel a strange mixture of concentration and confusion. They begin to shut out their surroundings. They scarcely hear the loud music in the room. The other voices, no matter how shrill, become blurred. More and more, their eyes, as they brush, begin to fasten and hold for long seconds, all but unblinking. They look away, and lower their heads. But always they return to it in a moment—to the bright focus of an inexplicable, onrushing intimacy.

Their conversation may drift unconsciously to comments about one another's bodies, the color of hair and eyes, the shape of hands. Then, gently testing, they are likely to touch in small ways. He brushes a cigarette ash from her arm. She picks a loose thread from his shoulder and then cannot resist guiding one stray lock of his hair back into place.

Their breathing becomes more rapid and shallow. They feel small muscular contractions. Their hands touch, and the electric wires are brushing again. There is scarcely any awareness of time or place, of past or future—only this all-electric, neon-lighted, star-burst, mind-blowing urgency of the present.

And before either realizes how or when it happens, before they can pause to reason or choose, the very deep yearning begins. . . .

This is the legendary all-electric meeting. Given a thousand names by a thousand poets, it has long been the culture's dream of how intimacy ought to start, of how love should introduce itself.

The same story has been told through millennia. It may be a tale of eternal love, as of Helen and Paris, or of Romeo and Juliet. Or it may be only an intense sensual episode, as in *Tom Jones* or the emotional wax museum of Ian Fleming's thrillers. In any case, it is the fabled green light for loving. It is quick and mystical and undeniable.

So entrenched is this idea that even in the 1970s most adolescent girls still wait secretly for a magic prince, who will awaken them from the sleep of unloving with one sensitive, sensitizing kiss. And every adolescent boy waits for the girl who will instantly recognize him as her mate—greet him with unqualified eagerness, welcome his every advance and return them with her own.

The idea is so indoctrinated by lifelong exposure to song and story, that few people ever fully abandon the expectation that it will happen one of these days. The belief remains hidden in the heart of nearly every man or woman—no matter how cynical they may become, how love-abused, how bitterly experienced, how chilled by time. Inwardly, they continue to look for the all-electric meeting as the initiatory signal that the time has come to pair. Some enchanted evening, as the old song puts it, we will see a stranger across a crowded room and ZAPWHAMPOW! *Love!*

It we were going to help people to understand intimate love and to achieve it, we had to deal with this fabled concept. We knew the feeling was expected. And we knew that it actually did occur. We knew that men and women looked for this electric feeling, this sudden chemistry as the intuitive starting gun for intimacy, as the confirmation of love beginning.

The concept is an ancient as recorded thought. The earliest Greeks invented little Eros to meet the expectations of the multitude. They put into his hands a bow and a quiver of love darts to dramatize the instancy of the experience. One twang of that bowstring, and any mortal, any god even, was left sighing and helpless before the power of love.

How was this idea viewed by the more sophisticated minds of Greece's Golden Age, by those who built the Acropolis and who so early anticipated almost every reach of twentieth-century thought?

An exemplary answer is Plato's principal writing on love, his fifth-century-B.C. dialogue, The Symposium. In this work, Plato has Aristophanes propound a theory of love's beginnings. Aristophanes disdains the logical arguments that make up the bulk of Platonic writing and turns instead to myth. In a time forgotten, he says, men were physically very different. Rather than being straight, upright creatures, men were roundish—each having four arms, four legs, and double most of their present characteristics. They were supermen, far more powerful and swift and daring than their descendants. Eventually, they actually dared to scale the heavens and assault the gods.

Zeus was outraged. Once the gods had repulsed

the heavenly attack, he decided to make sure that there could never be another. He hit upon the idea of weakening man by splitting him in half. Since that time, Aristophanes explains, people have zealously sought to find again their other halves.

Originally, he continues, there were three sexes—the all-man, the all-woman and the man-woman; now each human seeks to be reunited along these same patterns. "And when one of them meets with his other half," concludes Aristophanes, "... the pair are lost in an amazement of love and friendship and intimacy, and one will not be out of the other's sight, as I may say, even for a moment: these are the people who pass their whole lives together...."

It is interesting, first of all, to observe that Plato, who dared to probe the most difficult of all mankind's questions, and to consider the most unconventional answers, balked at explaining love. Instead, he resorted to myth, implying that love was a matter of unfathomable mystique.

Secondly, it is worth noting that his myth supports the Eros concept of love's beginning—the idea that one must wait patiently until the right partner is brought by the gods, that one need only to recognize the predestined partner when he comes.

Finally, Plato clearly implies support for what is probably the most dominant feeling about love in all literature and traditons. This is the concept that there is for each man or woman one Mister or Miss Right, who will eventually appear, and that when he or she at last arrives on the scene, intuitive electricity will flash to make the announcement.

Such thinking makes for charming poetry. But it makes a weak foundation for one's emotional life.

One result of this mystical view of love is that the vast majority of single people play a feverish romantic roulette, betting their lives on the poorest odds, armed with only gambler's hope, gambler's superstition, and gambler's guess, and without even knowing the rules that govern the game. Small wonder that so many end up losers.

Millions wait in loneliness for the magic electricity. Others find a momentary taste of it, are filled with hope, but later become nagged by doubts.

Often we hear such statements as this: "Gary travels all the time, Dr. Bach, and it's probably a good thing, because we build up so much tension when we're together. I don't even really approve of his work—buying small companies in trouble, so that his corporation can raid the assets. It seems unethical to me.

"We argue about religion, politics, my family, our friends, and about sex. But then he'll phone me from Detroit or Cleveland, and suddenly, there's the old magic, and we talk endlessly and sort of melt. This is what drives me crazy. Just when things are really bad and I think I have to get away from him, something happens to remind me of the fact I can't ignore. Whatever else is wrong, whatever I think, I *love* him."

This pair had conducted an affair for three years, and they had lived together for two of those years. They made each other miserable. Nevertheless, they clung to one another, dismissing all their misery on the grounds that they felt love, that the electricity was still strong from time to time. But in putting up with the misery, they developed a deep store of mutual resentment. We doubted that either would ever allow himself to behave in a genuine way. They came to the Institute because the dissonances between them were exhausting them. Yet they felt they dared not be separated from what electricity told them was the "rightness" of their match. Soon this couple parted company because they would rather split than be real; the reality of their true feelings caused them more conflict than they could stand.

The question remains: What is this electricity, this magic spell that makes so many dissonant pairs feel sure they are magically mated, and yet sentences them to a life without authenticity, a life of distorting and misrepresenting themselves in order to stay together? What is this aspect of love?

Both psychologists and lexicographers have long sought to define love. They generally content themselves with such synonyms as *affection, devotion*, and the like. And the only area of real agreement seems to be that love has many aspects. Perhaps chief among them are those of attraction, or electricity, and a brotherly kind of caring or concern.

The latter is easy to understand; people feel it from childhood with family and friends. But the attraction, the electricity, is more difficult to trace. It is hardly surprising that its explanations invoke winged gods, bows and arrows, and a library of myths of destiny.

The electricity generally makes its first appearance in adolescence. The young girl listens to romantic music or reads poetry, and fancies that she is emotionally aroused. The young man daydreams or loses himself in a somewhat pruriently interesting novel, and he experiences a similar feeling. The phenomenon is so well known, that it is the subject of endless stale jokes. The fact is that these two young people are really experiencing feelings of love, *but without any object*. They are erotically self-propelled, for no one else is there.

When the same girl gets a bit older, she goes to a rock concert; there are the Rolling Stones or Blood, Sweat and Tears. She takes her unattached feeling of love and applies it to a fantasy object. She sighs, she squeals, she experiences overt, physical sexual changes. And still, all this happens with no relationship at all, though now there exists a distant target. That afternoon, quite possibly, her young male counterpart has been going through a similar experience, while he was staring at the bare bosom and the suggestively maneuvered pelvis of a Swedish film star or a studied appraisal of the "Playmate of the Month" in *Playboy* magazine.

If these two adolescents now meet at a rock concert, and the self-generated electricity, reinforced by their unreal and distant relating, becomes supercharged by the frenzied and hypnotic music, sparks are sure to fly. As they dance, not touching but wanting to, their glances cannot separate. There is another all-electric meeting, and all their feelings pour out onto one another.

Question: Is this really love? Remember that their electricity existed before they ever met. In a sense, each of them was like a director seeking an actor for a part, and all the lines and stage directions had already been written. Yet when the part is filled, who can say this is not love?

At first, they are careful just to keep dancing and looking, and this avoids the disruption of the fantasy. The trip is good, and they want to keep it that way. Gradually, as they are forced to talk because of a break in the music, they allow an interaction to begin that bears at least some semblance to reality. Now the first anxiety appears. Its theme is, "Please don't spoil my dream."

So they are elaborately cautious, feeling their

way, delicately evading any dissonance, as if saying, "I'll take the part. Now what do I do?" Therefore, as he takes her home, their conversation is patterned with a view toward total safety. They met to the tune of music, so there is nothing safer than the subjects of music and records. And each is already playing a role simply because they are both members of the same subculture. They are both teenagers. They have many attitudes in common, as well as the same slang, the same kind of clothes. Each may depend upon remaining safe, because the other is too frightened to take off his mask.

And when he takes her to her door, and puts his arms around her and she reaches up for his kiss, it is really not a personal gesture but something of an anonymous mass embrace. For they are all entwined together—he and she, Ringo, Paul, Elke Sommer, Sir Lancelot, Elizabeth Taylor, Levi Strauss, Rod McKuen, the Hamilton High School yearbook, and the Lennon Sisters.

Most people are reluctant to admit it, but very similar phenomena can take place at any age, though later they are carefully rationalized by more sophisticated ideas. The process never really changes; it only becomes more complicated and more contaminated by adult experiences and possessions.

If the same pair had met ten years later, the principal changes would be in costume and props. He takes her, not to her home, but to his boat on the bay.

Neither wishes to see or share the realities of their two-hours-old union. Both, for example, are careful to avoid any reference to the fact that the place they are leaving is a singles bar, where both had arrived alone.

They keep the anonymous electricity going without much trouble. It is very romantic making love on the boat. And both are still cardboard characters for one another as they fall asleep.

Next morning, there are some problems. Reality threatens. Traditionally, in plays and novels, the threatening reality occurs at two fairly superficial levels, and these actually produce much less trouble than is commonly supposed. The real problem comes at a third level.

The first order of realities is simple and objective. She wakens to learn that Prince Charming gargles loudly after shaving, and is susceptible to stomach gas after an evening on the town. He, in turn, notes that when she has not worn her rollers to bed at night, she resembles a walking dust mop. He also observes something that had not been so obvious in the darkness and after lots of drinks the night before: when she is not wearing the dress with the tricky decolletage, she is not so generously endowed in the bosom.

But both are probably able to handle this sort of reality rather easily. For one thing, they are busy managing other problems.

The second traditional difficulty after the all-electric meeting also is not serious. It is the reaction: what-did-I-see-in-him? Since much of the electricity is self-generated, there is less excitement when the first intensity subsides. Yet at the same time the attraction has historical reasons within the individual, beyond feelings that permit love-without-an-object. That is, past experiences and affections tend to shape present ones. The other person offers a subtle set of cues that yield positive responses.

For example, the scar above his left eye is just like one that belonged to her school football hero. His crooked smile reminds her of the history teacher for whom she had a thing. He has that trick way of wrinkling his nose, like lovable old Uncle Albert. His speech has a New England twang that reminds her of those peaceful childhood summers in Maine. He is an architect, like Daddy. But he has a marvelously easy way of expressing himself, in contrast to her frustratingly silent and inexpressive father.

The list of desirable-appearing or compatible-appearing qualities is virtually infinite. A team of psychoanalysts, armed with a computer, would be needed to put all the factors together and weigh them for meaning. But the fact is, they add a positive charge.

The images of lovableness are also influenced by the traits of such public models as television, movie, or jet set personalities: Jackie Kennedy's or Audrey Hepburn's trim underfed looks and distant manners, Johnny Carson's dimply smile, Paul Newman's blue eyes. We caution pairers not to judge the attractiveness of a potential intimate by such stereotypes of lovableness. This is an important warning because, unconsciously, people in the first stages of getting together tend to place great emphasis on personality characteristics that resemble some stereotype.

This complex phenomenon is operating as the couple awakens on the boat the next morning. It moves them to make love again. But then the third reaction creeps in. It makes them smoke quite a lot as they talk, and decide, despite their hangover, to have a Bloody Mary. For it is a disturbing sense of anxiety. And it is an inevitable concomitant of an electric encounter. Why?

We and others, such as Rollo May, have been interested in what is known as the *over-mobilization theory* of emotions. This holds that when an individual wants something, he is likely to mobilize far more emotional energy than he really needs to get it.

This phenomenon influences male-female relationships. As soon as the electricity takes effect, a tantalizing hope rises inwardly. It is the feeling, "This could be love *NOW*," and the effects are profound.

Overmobilization certainly enlarged the reactions, physical and emotional, of the electrified pair who met at the cocktail party at the beginning of this chapter and could not keep their hands away from each other. The same force generated enough emotional energy in the couple on the boat to send them to bed immediately and to make love again in the less romantic light of the morning after. In all such cases, overmobilization also magnifies all the attendant emotions, chief among them anxiety.

"This could be love NOW," is at once a promise and a threat. The promise is that an intimate longing may be about to be fulfilled. The threat is that it will not be.

This intimate threat, this anxiety of love, is a complex matter. Primarily, it is a fear that the other person will not feel love. But underneath this fear lies a web of other fears—of being used, exploited, manipulated; of being swallowed up and controlled; of being kept at a distance or being drawn too close; of becoming dependent or of being too much depended upon. The list is a long one. Its salient items vary with the individual. The greatest fear, of course, is the fear of losing love. And the greater the affection grows, the greater grows that fear.

We have learned that, even more important than understanding the individual anxieties of love, is understanding the choice that must be made the moment these feelings appear. For from the first hints of fear, the would-be lover is at a crossroad. He must decide how to manage that fear. There are two basic ways. The first is the courting way—denying the fear, glossing over the realities that produce it. It is the smooth way at first, but in the end it brings mounting discomfort, and is not likely to lead to intimate love.

The alternative is the pairing way. It confronts and deals with the anxiety-making realities. Outwardly, it may appear unsettling, but inwardly it relieves the fears and tensions, and is the psychologically sound path to intimacy. The time to share fears and to confront the possibilities of conflict is from the start. We warn lovers against the courtship dictum "Let's love now and fight later." From the very beginning, the stereotypes of lovableness should be confronted and exposed as unnecessary. Instead, the unique realities of each new relationship should be focused on.

Almost invariably, the courting way is not chosen consciously, but tends to be an unconscious reaction in favor of what appears to be immediately safe and reassuring. How can such an important choice be made with little or no awareness? How can a potential intimate recognize the self-illusion? Only through understanding the fears of love can an aware decision be made in favor of reality——and the intimate longing be fulfilled.

6

Of people,
images,
and things

THE typical method by which people deal with
their early fears of love is *imaging*: choosing an
attractive way of presenting oneself and what one
has to offer.

Some imaging is inevitable and harmless. People
who seek love want to be at their best. They enjoy
taking extra pains with their grooming and like to
summon up all the wit and charm they can command. They like to show off their skills, their knowl-
edgeability about choosing wine, perhaps, or their
backhand at tennis. They revel in the opportunity to
stand up tall and hold in the abdomen and watch
how much a potential intimate admires their most
lovable qualities. It is very satisfying to make the
most of one's attributes.

But another aspect of imaging is a barrier to intimacy. Feeling the electricity and the anxiety that
follows, the courter seeks to solidify his acceptability. One of the safest ways to accomplish this is to

present himself not as an individual, but as one of an acceptable group.

This flocking-together is most noticeable among teen-agers. They want to dress alike, talk alike, wear their hair alike, and express similar attitudes. They are actually playing out one form of matching. In effect, they say to a potential intimate: "You are most likely to love a type who looks and acts like a with-it teen-ager. I want to show you that I am a with-it teen-ager. Then I will fit that frame of preference and you will accept me into it."

Teen-age façades change like quicksilver, but their purpose remains the same. At this writing, bell-bottoms, long hair, and work-type clothes are in on the campus. Twenty-five years ago, it was the left-over war dress of flight jackets and combat boots.

Adults adopt much the same group colorations, and not only to initiate sexual relationships. A man who wants to borrow money confronts his banker in a dark, pin-stripe suit and conservative tie. He, too, is dealing with anxiety. His silent message is, "Look. You can tell I belong to the world of respectable, responsible people, can't you? Trust me."

In the male-female introduction, the member-of-the-group image is often conveyed by emphasizing one's occupational role. Young medical students going to a university dining room for lunch keep their white coats on and let their stethoscopes hang out. The image is a message. In this case it is supposed to be, "I am a doctor type, trustworthy, educated, earnest, good catch, and I can tell quite a bit about you just by looking at you."

Often the image-message is verbal. For men and women soon learn what makes them part of an attractive group in the eyes of the opposite sex. Writers and psychologists, for example, do not take long to find that the mere mention of their professions usually evokes a fairly strong positive or negative reaction. For such a role promises to offer understanding, highly attractive to some, highly repellent to others. Other occupational roles carry connotations of glamour, sophistication, money, kindness.

The imager really presents himself, not as a person, but as a symbol. Many people dislike cocktail parties because the rapid procession of meetings encourages people to present themselves as mere symbols. Much of the first cocktail-party exchange really means: "Here is my symbol. (Executive, glamour girl, hippie, etc.) Does it interest and attract you? Can your own symbol relate to it?"

A common reason given for the dislike of cocktail parties is, "They are phony" (dehumanizing). The insight is accurate. They *are* dehumanizing. They are made so because typically, it is not people who are sipping the drinks, but impersonal symbols. For the core fact about symbolizing oneself is that, in doing so, one does not present oneself as a person.

This phenomenon is one of the most important factors that keep relationships nonintimate. Only *people* can achieve intimacy.

No implication is intended that men and women actually regard other people as totally inanimate objects. The idea is just that nonintimates do not always see people as whole, as having lives of real fear and wanting and hope. Often this perception of people occurs because the viewer wants little information about them. No one wishes to be swamped by intimacy. If one has plenty of warmly responsive friends and intimates, there certainly is no need to seek more intimacy from one's boss, secretary, TV repairman, or fellow-guest at a cock-tail party.

But nonintimates usually *choose* consistently to see others in terms of their roles, their functions, and their most superficial meanings.

A person who is afflicted with this habit is very probably not unfeeling. He would be shocked if he saw a wall collapse on a crowd in the streets. But the point is that he regards human beings as not much more than things. In a technical paper, the senior author of this book has described this mode in human relationships as *thinging*. When a person is *thinged*, only one aspect, or group of aspects, of his existence is recognized as real.

When someone "things" another person, he sees that other person principally as an object, especially if the other person is a stranger who serves primarily as a handicap: the fellow who is ahead in line at the bank, the motorcycle cop who restrains one's driving speed, or the man who gets first to a waiting cab.

People who are thinged can also be facilitators. In this case they are like machines, or extensions of machines, that make things available to others. This is known as *functional segmentalization;* only that part of the thinged person that performs a desired function is recognized. The gas station attendant becomes an extension of a machine that fills the tank, washes the windshield, and fills out the charge slip. The supermarket checker is regarded as part of a machine that adds up the bill and puts the gro-ceries in a paper bag.

People can also be segmentalized in much broader terms. Myra, who is secretary to the boss, does seem like a person. One knows that she has two children, that her husband drinks and can't hold a job, and that her mother is ill in Seattle. But there is no real bond with her. If one knows her weakness for choco-late fudge, or her delight in a toy for her children, one can manipulate her so as to help get the boss's attention and favor.

Thinging always involves a utilitarian aspect. Typically a thinger in a restaurant thinks about the waitress: "Serve me my cup of coffee and don't bug me with your headache or your sore feet."

Obviously intimacy is impossible with a person who is segmentalized. Intimacy requires the accept-ance of another as whole. Also, thinging requires illuding oneself by shutting out the nonuseful part of the person. (The waitress with the tired feet may be a Ph.D. student whose scholarship funds have run out or a mother of three whose husband has desert-ed her. The thinger does not want to know such facts.)

Finally, a most provocative phenomenon. When someone things another, he also automatically things himself. To the checker at the supermarket the thing-er is a machine buying groceries and giving mon-ey. The prostitute who is being used sees her client as a body and a wallet.

So when a woman treats her date as a thing who takes her to places and entertains her, she should not be surprised if he treats her as a thing, too, perhaps a rubber stamp of approval. He may win approval as a symbol. But as a person, he is not even recognized. And he cannot hope for intimacy while he remains a symbol.

Vicki is a shy, quiet girl with a very good figure. She feels that her form is her principal way of attracting male interest and approval. So she buys her dresses very small, and delights whenever fash-ion calls for higher hemlines.

When Dennis, the newest office bachelor, asks her

to a party, she buys a new dress, tight and short. And after a great deal of reassurance from the saleslady that, "After all, it's what they're wearing," she buys it in the no-bra *décolletage* model.

Vicki is symbolizing herself as a sexy girl. Dennis hovers over her all evening, but it is not surprising that he reads into her symbol more than she intends. For, contrary to her image, Vicki's sexuality is rigidly suppressed by burdensome taboo feelings.

When Dennis acts on his interpretation of her symbol, as he takes her home, Vicki is genuinely outraged.

"Please, Dennis," she explodes. "Please take your hand out of there! I don't know what you think I am! I want you to know my brother is a priest, and I go to early-morning mass every day."

Dennis is first startled and then angry, as if to say, "But it says right here in your advertisement—" Were there a Better Business Bureau of dating, he would write a stinging letter of complaint in the morning. He feels swindled, affronted, gulled.

Not only had Vicki presented herself to Dennis as a thing, a torso: She had revealed almost nothing personal about herself, other than her cleavage, during the entire evening. So she should not really have been surprised when Dennis treated her as a torso and thinged her as a sex object. She also thinged Dennis by seeing him as a stamp of social approval and an admission card to the party.

Thinging is perhaps the most obvious symptom of exploitation. It is certainly the most likely way to make a reasonable, perceptive person feel exploited. And when he feels exploited, he becomes angry and will probably try hard to make the exploiter aware of him as a whole person. This accounts for some of Dennis' angry response to Vicki's behavior.

One of the most venerable principles of psychotherapy is that there are few victims who are not also victimizers. Dennis really chose Vicki as his date for the party because of her physical appearance. So when she does a good job in acting out the role in which he placed her, he should not feel so put upon.

Their thinging game could have been broken up almost at once, if either Vicki or Dennis had opened up as a person, and thereby demanded authentic behavior from the other. Both were guilty of suppressing their realities, and thereby arranged their own failure, which took place the moment something real—in this case, Dennis's hand—intruded.

More often, imaging is more subtle, and a longer time passes before it comes into undeniable conflict with reality. The story of Phil and Dorothy is a case in point.

Phil is a bright banker, 36, who is a bit tight-fisted. He was charmed by a new young teller named Dorothy, 24. Dorothy was also attracted to Phil, but gave him no hint of her interest.

Since Phil is not a stellar conversationalist, he had to rely on imaging, he thought, to interest Dorothy. He began to tell her of his glamorous lunch, cocktail, and party contacts with the bank's many show-business clients. Her eyes lighted up every time he told another tale. After some weeks, he asked her for a date, and she accepted.

Phil dislikes expensive restaurants. But realizing how much glamor imaging he had done, he decided that he really ought to take Dorothy to a glamor dinner. Dorothy was thrilled. She also imaged, by posing as a gourmet and trying to order a very complete meal, with quite a few delicacies, while Phil secretly shuddered at the tab.

It was only 10 o'clock when they finished coffee.

"Well, what do we do now?" Dorothy asked, a little breathless with anticipation. Phil smiled the knowing, confident smile of his glamor image, although he felt financial disaster approaching, and took Dorothy to a night club.

On their second date, he called for her, with the plan of a simple dinner and then a movie. When he arrived, she was dressed to the teeth. Excitedly she said, "What wonderful surprise do you have for me tonight."

For a moment, Phil hesitated. She was so very pretty, so very fresh. No such lovely girl had ever been his date before. He wanted to tell her that all the glamorous entertaining that he did in the interests of the bank were paid for by the bank. But then the anxious feeling rose up. What would happen to all his glamour, the asset that he assumed had attracted her? He had to keep his image. And one more outing would not destroy him.

For the next few weeks, there was another and another and another restaurant tab. Phil suffered every time he signed another bill. He felt in an even tighter bind when Dorothy confided that she had always felt unworthy with men, and that they had treated her as if she were. She told him how wonderful it was of him to show her so much respect and treat her so much like a lady.

Now he feared that if he took her to less elegant places, she would think he had lost that respect. But he had incorrectly interpreted what she said to him. She was talking about his respectful style with her. Ironically, she was becoming uncomfortable because she began to feel that he wanted her merely as a doll-like companion on the town. And so she started spending too much on new clothes to match what she thought was his doll image of her.

Just once, she would have liked to be alone with him, walking and talking, but she assumed that his romantic interest in her was small. They saw each other rather infrequently, because he could not stand what he thought was the necessary expense.

Then an accident dropped reality in their laps. One night, at dinner, he reached for his wallet, and it was not there. (We shall let Freudians make what they will of Phil's slip.) But Dorothy had some money and paid the check. It took all she had.

"I'll pay you back, of course," he said.

"No," she replied. "You've been so good to me. Let me say thanks this way."

"No, I really want to go back to my place and get my wallet. Then I can pay you back, and we can also have money for the rest of the evening."

Her generous gesture and directness emboldened her. Suddenly she felt like the hostess, instead of the poor waif being fed.

"No, this is *my* evening," she insisted, "I'm out of money. But if you don't mind coming to my place, I have some Scotch. Would you mind?"

"Mind?" he asked, and was shocked into making a real statement. "That's what I've really wanted to do ever since the first day you came to work!"

Phil had symbolized himself as tour guide and generous benefactor who had no demands upon Dorothy. In turn, he thinged her as a puppet who could do nothing for him, except express gratitude and delight at his generosity. Phil made himself a thing, and forced Dorothy to treat him as a thing. They began to feel tense and dissatisfied in one another's company. And since their relationship was really between two images, not people, it could not grow. It was static. Both began to have the sense that it was likely to wane from this state. And they were right.

A lucky accident—or was it completely an accident and not an unconscious act?—forced them to dare being real. Without money, Phil had lost his role. And when Phil had to change, to stop being Daddy Warbucks, he was momentarily without a tight role to step into.

In that moment, Dorothy had the courage to push past her own fear and snap up the role of giver. Psychology calls the phenomenon *role-reversal;* it is one sign of a healthy, whole personality to be able to manage such a change when there is real need for it. It stops thinging.

Phil might have fought to hold on to his old giver role, if the accident had occurred once the relationship was more firmly established and he had come to be more dependent on it for his own security. But by her reversal, Dorothy let him give up the role. She was really saying, "I like being with you, even if you can't be Lord Bountiful. Let me prove it by taking you to my house and just talking to you, being with you, without your giving me any bribes."

Dorothy thereby eliminated Phil's anxiety that he was desirable to her only as a thing, an entertainment fountain. He could now be a person, and he became one that evening by taking instead of giving.

Later, we shall see that imaging can also be broken, in oneself or in another person, by conscious design, which we call reality-testing technique. But if no accident happens until a couple is more deeply involved, intimacy may be denied for a lifetime.

Let us look now at another couple. The surface of their relationship and its inner functioning can be examined through a *quadrilog,* a four-voiced conversation of the sort that is characteristic of courting-style couples as they first meet. The spoken thoughts *should* reveal the state of the relationship. But they do not. For they are not real. Only the unvoiced inner thoughts are. These courters are fencing in the dark. They are achieving no real contact. Where the relationship should emerge, there is a virtual blank.

The introduction of this couple takes place at a public camera club that also serves as a singles meeting place. He is an old member, and she is new. They have eyed one another for obvious reasons. She is a very attractive young woman in her early thirties, and she is almost six feet tall. He is a plain, but wholesome-looking man in his late thirties, and he is six feet five inches tall. It is now the coffee break time.

THEY SAY	THEY THINK
HE: Well, you're certainly a welcome addition to our group.	*Can't I ever say something clever?*
SHE: Thank you. It certainly is friendly and interesting.	*He's cute.*
HE: My friends call me Stretch. It's left over from my basketball days. Silly, but I'm used to it.	*It's safer than saying my name is David Stein.*
SHE: My name is Candy.	*At least my nickname is. He doesn't have to hear Hortense O'Brien.*
STRETCH: What kind of	*Why couldn't a girl*

THEY SAY	THEY THINK
camera is that?	*named Candy be Jewish. It's only a nickname, isn't it?*
CANDY: Just this old German one of my uncle's. I borrowed it from the office.	*He could be Irish. And that camera looks expensive.*
STRETCH: May I? (He takes her camera, brushing her hand and then tingling with the touch.) Fine lens. You work for your uncle?	*Now I've done it. Brought up work.*
CANDY: Ever since college.	*So okay, what if I only went for a year?*
It's more than being just a secretary. I get into sales, too.	*If he asks what I sell, I'll tell him anything except underwear.*
STRETCH: Sales? That's funny. I'm in sales, too, but mainly as an executive. I run our department.	*Is there a nice way to say used cars? I'd better change the subject.*
I started using cameras on trips. Last time it was in the Bahamas. I took—	*Great legs! And the way her hips move—*
CANDY: Oh! Do you go to the Bahamas, too? I love those islands.	*So I went just once, and it was for the brassiere manufacturers convention. At least we're off the subject of jobs.*
STRETCH:	*She's probably really been around. Well, at least we're off the subject of jobs.*

THEY SAY	THEY THINK
I did a little underwater work there last summer. Fantastic colors. So rich in life.	*And lonelier than hell.*
CANDY:	*Look at that build. He must swim like a fish. I should learn.*
I wish I'd had time when I was there. I love the water.	*Well, I do. At the beach, anyway, where I can wade in and not go too deep.*

In just a few minutes, these two have set a pattern of imaging from which it is going to be hard to retreat. After the meeting, they have a drink and talk until the bar closes, matching, matching, and matching—politics, tastes in clothes, houses, cars, all the impersonal things. Their similarity in height gives them a sense of destined sameness that makes them feel as a unit apart from the world. They forget the world. They go to his apartment, and the sex is so good that they feel very bound to each other.

They spend the weekend together, and by the time it is over they both feel they are in love, and say so. It is the electric magic. It is a fairytale, a dream realized. They are enchanted. They ask few questions of one another, for they do not want to commit themselves to specific answers.

One of the matters they scrupulously avoid is religion. The difference became apparent, of course, as soon as last names were exchanged. But they smoothed over the problems quickly. Wasn't all that a thing of the past?

"Good Lord," says Stretch, "*Abie's Irish Rose*" was fifty years ago. People think differently now."

"Of course," agrees Candy. "You know, the Church has made the rules easier for all kinds of interfaith things. If the O'Briens can't be as liberal as the Pope—" she laughs.

"My family is very liberal," says Stretch. "You know, sometimes I'm afraid my father is really a Socialist," he winks. "No kidding. He really is! Hey, Listen! Why are we talking this way? We're not getting married or anything, are we?"

"I mean what I said," replies Candy. "I'd never marry a man until I'd lived with him."

A few weeks later, they are going stronger than ever. Candy tells him: "I couldn't keep quiet about you when I visited home the other night. My mother got all excited. She wants to meet you."

"I'd like to meet her," says Stretch.

"Well, you will some day. I told her you had to work nights a lot, so you couldn't come to dinner next Friday."

"But I'm off Friday."

"Oh, I just thought, well, it's better not to just yet. I mean, it's like I was trapping you. I've never brought a fellow home for dinner since high school. I mean, I sort of like to keep things just for us, at least for now."

"I know what you mean. I mentioned you at home, too, and Ma said the same thing, and I ducked it. You know, it really gets very heavy, the whole family scene. I sort of feel it's our business right now, nobody else's."

Neither will tell the other the anxiety they experience and, to some extent, aren't even aware of—the knowledge of what will happen when a girl named

O'Brien is presented to the Steins, and vice versa. They know that pressure will be applied by both families. They are apprehensive of the commotion that will presumably follow. In effect, they deny an internal anxiety that already exists.

These illusions could not sustain themselves without the courting-style device of collusion. Each wants to maintain the other's evasive illusion. Both must work hard to avoid piercing the other's image, for if they did, they would increase their fear of losing love. They know they are not being honest, but each rationalizes his behavior as "understanding." The fear of losing their new-found love is so strong that they actually help one another avoid any unpleasant truths that might threaten their "bliss."

The truth is that Candy's family and friends would disapprove of Stretch. She would be embarrassed. Stretch feels the same. Both families are narrow-minded concerning religion. And Candy and Stretch are the children of their parents.

Stretch slips once, when he says, after Candy has nursed him through a cold, "You know, you're very Jewish." Candy slips, too, when she says another time, "You're not like other Jews I know."

Both cooperate to smooth over the slips. Each resents the reference, but says inwardly that it is understandable and really a compliment. It just doesn't feel like one, and each is really very sensitive about what seems at heart like a slight.

What they are now experiencing, as both avoid their families and former friends and crowd themselves into a very narrow world for two is called *accommodation.*

Accommodation is an extension of imaging. It is a further, more deeply felt way of crowding oneself into another's picture of what is lovable. Candy and

Stretch are denying their real wishes—for example, to be with friends and family again—as a way of avoiding the frightening reality that might make them separate. They are having to lop off important parts of themselves to keep one another's love. It is destructive business, and it makes intimacy slip further and further out of their grasp. For each time one of them denies part of his emotions for the sake of the other, denies real wishes and hungers, he resents the other for making him pay the price. The realities can be hidden indefinitely. But intimacy lies buried with them.

As so often happens, accident of a sort intervened to force the realities out for Candy and Stretch, in an ironic way. Deny it though she would, Candy was at heart very loyal to her Catholicism. Somehow it had not really occurred to Stretch that Candy did not take The Pill. But, as the psychotherapist at our Institute later suggested, perhaps it had. In any event, Candy became pregnant. Both sought our help. They were shown how to be real with each other, got married, and are slowly working out the painful realities of their differences.

Since accommodation is a most popular way of avoiding fears that prevent intimacy, it deserves a closer look.

7

The accommodations of love

IN the beginning, it seems only politeness. No one wants to appear indifferent to a partner's wishes, after all, or self-centered about his own. It is only the courteous thing to put another's comfort or pleasure first.

So no alarm bells go off when accommodation begins to meet the intimate anxiety of hiding real feelings from a partner. And once accommodation begins, it is hard to stop.

Will and Carol, who have been dating for some weeks, have had an exhilarating day on the beach. Their dates have been good-time expeditions, and the conversation has been limited to trifling subjects. They have been physically affectionate, which was very stimulating to both, but until now they have not gone to bed.

At the beach they touched a great deal, in the water and on the sand, and both became excited. They had dinner at a seaside place, and a couple of drinks raised their sexuality and frankness. Will finally asked Carol to spend the night at his apartment, and, she agreed. Impatiently, they started the long drive home.

Half way, they began to feel the fatigue that follows too much sun and sea and wine. It is Sunday, and both must be at work early next day. They begin to regret their plan—but only in secret. Now their real personalities start to show.

WILL (stretching behind the wheel, he groans just a little, uncomfortably):

CAROL:
Is something wrong?

WILL:
Oh, nothing much. (Bravely) I guess I got some sunburn. Quite a lot in fact.

CAROL:
Well, I wish you'd have let me put some lotion on you. I asked you, remember? Maybe if you put something on it as soon as you get home . . .

WILL (a little annoyed. He wanted sympathy, not medical advice. He frequently wants sympathy for his many minor complaints.):
Yes, I will. I'm not sure it's just sunburn, actually. I sort of have a cramp in my back, and I—

CAROL:
Is that the right time on the dashboard clock?

WILL (more annoyed):
Why? Are you very tired? You really won't be getting any sleep tonight, I'm afraid, by the time we get home. I'll be all right, but—

CAROL (looking at him to try to read his expression):

Well, you won't get any more sleep than I do. (She forces a smile.) Aren't you tired? I'll be fine.

WLL:
Well, if you don't *want* to, Carol—I mean, I'll understand. I want to, but I don't *have* to, tonight.

CAROL (her competitive streak showing through):
Maybe *I* have to. (She forces a smile.) You can't get out of it.

WILL:
As if I want to!

Both would really prefer to go home and to sleep. But they are trapped. They do not want to seem inadequate for one another. When they finally reach Will's apartment, they are sleepy and dulled, but they proceed. Now they have been having intercourse for several minutes. They are tired, but they continue to embrace with all the show of passion they can muster.

THEY SAY	THEY THINK
WILL: Carol, darling—	*I hope she can come soon. My back is ready to break, and I don't know how much longer I can wait. What if I lose control? Maybe if I show more passion, she'll get more excited.*
CAROL: Oh, Will, darling!	*Oh! My sunburn!*
WILL: I love you, Carol!	*My left leg is cramping.*
CAROL: Yes, yes!	*I can't come. I know it. I'm too tired.*

THEY SAY	THEY THINK
WILL: I could go on all night!	*Please come. You said you could. I don't want to lose control. I remember what you said about men who were selfish and immature in bed.*
CAROL: Yes! Yes! Harder!	*Well I can't go on all night I'm losing all sensation. I wish you'd just go ahead and come. Please.*
WILL (complying): Like this?	*As if it wasn't tough enough to hold back before. Two plus two are four; four plus four are eight. Eight and eight—*
CAROL: Yes! More!	*I think he's weakening. If he'll only come, he won't think I'm frigid. I know I'll come with him another time. Maybe I could even fake it. I bet he couldn't tell.*
WILL: Oh! Carol, I—Can—can you—make—it?	*Please say yes. I'm at the end of my rope.*
CAROL: Yes! Yes I can! The minute you—do!	*Damn, I'm closing up or something. It's starting to hurt. I'll just have to fake and hope for the best.*
WILL: I hate to have it end.	*Thank heaven! But for her sake, I'll hang on another minute. Sixty-four and—*
CAROL: Now, darling! Oh,	*For pity's sake, get it over*

THEY SAY	THEY THINK
Will!	*with. Is he? I'm almost sure. Well, I'll try to be convincing.*
WILL: AH!!	*At last!*
CAROL: OH!!	*Hallelujah. I thought he never would.*

(THERE IS A MOMENT
OF SILENT RELIEF)

WILL: Did you?	
CAROL: Did I ever? Was it nice for you, Will?	*That's not an actual lie. And I will some other time. I really hope he liked me.*
WILL: Did I like it? Silly girl! Was it really all right for you?	*I wonder if she'd be awfully hurt if I just went to sleep. Burke is coming in for that meeting very early tomorrow.*
CAROL: Oh, Will. (She sighs.) I knew you'd be a real man. Are you always so strong?	*I hope he doesn't want to talk long. I have to do something with my hair before I can go to work.*
WILL: I think I would be for you. I didn't get too rough for you at the end, I hope?	*She wants to talk a while. Well, I don't really mind.*
CAROL: No, you'd never hurt me. But you are quite a man.	*He wants to talk. Oh, well. He would. He's really a fine lover, but it's so late.*
WILL (beams): Am I? Of course, what else could	*I'm glad she feels that way. I can see how im-*

THEY SAY	THEY THINK
I be with that wonderful body of yours? (He strokes it.)	*portant sex is for her.*
CAROL: And I love *your* body. (She caresses him.) Most men just want to go to sleep.	*I know I'll need at least an hour for my hair. It's so salty.*
WILL: I'm not most men. Besides, I've waited so long to touch you.	*She really is special. If only Burke weren't coming so early—I don't want to seem crude. Women need afterplay; it says so in the books.*
CAROL: Oh, Will! (She reproves.)	*I know I'm supposed to want this, and it's sweet. But the time is— Hey! I really like for him to touch me there, but—hey!*
WILL: I'm not hurting you?	
CAROL: No, I like that.	*Except at three in the morning. I really should return the gesture.*
WILL: Oh, Carol; You'll turn me on. Oh, Carol—	*It is now three A.M. Burke is due at eight-thirty. Maybe she's trying to tell me she needs more. I wonder if I could—*
CAROL: Do you want to again, dear?	*I may as well hear the news.*
WILL: I want to, but you must be so tired—	*What can I say?*

THEY SAY	THEY THINK
CAROL: I'm not too tired if you need me—	*What am I saying? But after all he's said about cool, unsexed women—*
WILL: Really?	*Does that mean she expects more?*
CAROL: Really.	*I knew once wouldn't be enough for him.*
WILL: Darling. Do you like this?	*It's a flat offer. I can't refuse.*
CAROL: Oh, yes. And do *you* like *this?*	*I do, but why now?*
WILL: Oh . . .	*If she keeps that up, I just might make it.*
CAROL: Darling, now!	*Let's get it over with.*
WILL: You're wonderful, the way you can say things right out so frankly. Is this what you have in mind?	*Let's get it over.*
CAROL: Oh . . .	*And he'll expect me to come.*
WILL: Oh . . .	*And she'll expect me to come.*
CAROL: Aaah . . .	*There's no choice. I'll just have to fake it again.*
WILL: Aaah . . .	*I'm sure I can't come. It's a miracle that I can do anything at all. I wonder if she could tell if I faked coming?*

It is fairly obvious what is going to happen next. A mutually unwanted sexual experience is about to end in a mutually nonexistent orgasm. And mutually unreal pleasure will surely be expressed.

This is the first and most superficial result of the accommodating behavior of Will and Carol. They did not want to fail one another's expectations. So they disregarded their own wishes, and tried to behave as their partners seemed to wish. In so doing, each gave false clues. Each created an illusion, a false perception of reality, in the other's mind.

On this superficial level, the situation is merely ironic. But it has deeper levels, and these bode trouble ahead.

The high impact of the initiatory act in a relationship is of utmost importance. The first date, the first dance, the first fight, the first sex carry great weight in setting up a style and pattern of future relating. This is particularly true when an act represents a change from insecurity and isolation to acceptance and security. It is easy to see how the moment of sexual acceptance is unusually impactful. It is usually the most dramatic sign of acceptance.

Initiatory acts are therefore most likely to be accompanied by anxiety. That anxiety is likely to be dealt with by an effort to disregard one's own feelings, and to accommodate to what one *thinks* one's partner wants. So it is probable that partners will not be very authentic during initiatory acts.

Will and Carol have initiated a pattern of a highly sexed relationship. Each feels obligated to offer sex often, and to accept any offer enthusiastically. Sex between the two is likely to develop a component of resentment. Each is committed to be a highly sexed *thing.* It will be extremely difficult to back down from this role later.

On a still deeper level accommodation can reflect potent forces in the personality, forces that may not even be recognized by the partners in their own minds. This actually happened with Will and Carol. We know because they later came as a couple to one of our group sessions.

Their conversation on the way home from the beach leaves clues for the therapist, which we later confirmed. Will's remarks, such as his physical complaints, suggest a touch of *Mother's-little-boy style.* Carol's urge to keep up with Will's nonexistent sexual appetite suggests what proved to be a mild competitive feeling toward men, with some resentment and fear of male dominance.

Both were insecure about their sexual adequacy and this insecurity had actually helped to bring them together in the first place. For Will was mild and not threatening to Carol. And Carol struck an independent note, which was important because Will did not want a dependent woman. He wanted a little taking care of.

When they realized how tired they would be before they could get to Will's apartment, both became anxious about how sexually adequate they would be. Will pleaded sunburn and a back cramp, hoping Carol might back off. He could not do the retreating because he was not sufficiently confident. He was afraid that his masculinity would be doubted.

Carol was in a similar situation, Also, her competitive feeling toward men was aroused by Will's uncertainty. Feeling threatened by the male, she needed to seize the upper hand when opportunity knocked.

The accommodation that led to sex that neither

wanted also masked these deeper problems. And then the experience itself confirmed their fears.

Will was sometimes premature in his sexual climax. Carol knew that she was capable of orgasm only some of the time; but never when fatigued. Will had difficulty controlling himself. Carol failed. The initiatory act carried a threat of sexual failure for both of them. It also began a worrisome belief that the sexual demand of the partner was going to be too high. The final mock "mutual" orgasm set the confirming seal on illusion created by accommodation.

Other factors in their relationship had a binding effect, however, over the next months. They loved each other. But one unpleasant experience after another was triggered by feelings of inadequacy and guilt. The affair was going downhill when they came to learn pairing methods.

As they opened up, it became apparent that many of their frustrating scenes were devices by which one partner set the other at a distance. This happened when the setting suggested a sexual demand might be made and could not be met adequately.

Similarly, each felt (resentfully) that he or she had to perform what "any man" or "any woman" is supposed to be capable of. They had one bad fight after Will needed curtains made, and Carol, an unskilled woman with a needle, felt she had to volunteer. Another came when Will baited Carol unmercifully as soon as she asked him to make some repairs which he did not know how to do.

Eventually, Will and Carol learned to level with each other in pairing style. Carol asked Will for less sexual demand, and Will admitted that he had the same desire. They then could tell each other some of

their real feelings about sex and their fears of inadequacy.

Traditional therapists would be likely to say that
Carol and Will needed psychoanalysis. We made the
decision that this was unnecessary, and once Will
and Carol learned pairing technique, they were able
to develop mutual trust. When they could depend
on a flow of real feelings between one another, their
anxieties were sharply reduced. Since each knew
now exactly what the other asked, and what feelings
their behavior produced in the other, neither felt
threatened any longer.

We did not probe into their individual histories
deeply. They dealt with their problem by facing
their relationship in the here-and-now. And their
repeated success in dealing with present problems
and threats realistically, reduced their anxieties.
Mild neurotic symptoms began to disappear.

Good pairing technique often yields such benefi-
cial effect on the whole personality, for it improves
the basic style of dealing with *all* others. Will reported, for example, this his new ability to be genuine
with both his boss and his customers had made him
more effective in his business life, and put him in
line for promotion.

Part of the value of the pairing technique is that it
meets potentially complex problems *at the moment
they arise*, while they are still relatively simple. During Will and Carol's first few moments in bed, for
example, they might have handled their problem
simply and effectively.

Because what they are thinking is now close to
what they say, there is no need to peer into their
minds by way of a quadrilog. The exchange is authentic.

WILL:

It's really a fine thing to have you alone with me like this and be close to you. But I'm so damned bushed that I'm afraid I'm going to be a rotten lover for you.

CAROL:

I know what you mean. Right now I'm about as lively as a dead flounder. My hair is a mess, and I can't help thinking how I'll ever make it to the office tomorrow. You know, I'm not Cleopatra or anything in bed, Will, and it's important to me not to disappoint you. Because I really want you, and I very much hope that you want me.

WILL:

Hey, stop running yourself down! You'd turn any man on. Every time I've touched you, I've dreamed about being close this way. But maybe we should both admit we're human enough to be too tired, and that we don't want to spoil this first time?

CAROL:

If you'll let me come back here again, I'll admit it. Otherwise, I'll have to try and trap you right now.

WILL (putting his arms around her):

You're really something special, Carol. It's my fault for not getting us home earlier. Say, listen: you know, I sometimes wake up pretty early. It's just possible that could happen. We'd both be a little bit rested—

CAROL:

Will you wake me up if you're awake? I could give you coffee—or something. (She smiles in the dark.)

WILL:
Well, if I do wake up early, I'll shave before I wake you.

CAROL:
Will?

WILL:
Yes.

CAROL:
Why don't you set the alarm, for early?

This exchange straightens out many potential problems quickly and is therefore a good pairing conversation. Its crucial quality is the direct expression of authentic feelings.

To say that transparency of feelings is what lovers require in order to become intimate is about as useful as saying that poor people would be better off if they had more money. Fear and anger often keep people from knowing what their innermost feelings are, or from risking the open expression of them. Such expression is not really possible until the individual has been freed of hard-to-identify intimate anxieties. One cannot be genuine until one feels safe.

The greatest problem in pairing classes has been to reduce the anxiety that springs up at the first sign of love, and grows deeper and more complex as love grows and separation becomes more of a threat. We have found solutions to the problem, and many of these should be learned *before* the first moment of contact with a potential intimate. This prevents the pollution of the relationship by fear and unrealistic formalism.

8

The
intimate eye
and the
guesting heart

MAKING new pairing contacts depends on the development of one personal quality as a successful pairer. We call that quality valency* and we borrow the term from chemistry. Chemically speaking, valency is the combining capacity of an atom. In pairing terms, valency is the combining capacity of a person. The key is the exposing of genuine, here-and-now feelings to another. These tend to elicit genuine responses from the other, to create a reassuring sense of reality, an up-to-the-minute, valid flow of information. If fair questions are asked, the real emotional state of the relationship can be clearly known.

With confidence in the pairing system, a potential intimate automatically raises his valency. He learns

* We do not mean here the *valence* of Kurt Lewin's psychological field theory, where it refers to the attracting or repelling power of motivational goals.

that pairing techniques bring out pleasant surprises, unexpected interest and depth in others. So he is less likely to treat people as stereotypes, to make them into things and to deal with them from a distance. He is curious. He wants to get closer. His romantic preconceptions of what a partner ought to be are replaced by open-mindedness. So are his illusions of walking into some magic room to find the all-electric eyes of his perfect match, his *Right One*.

The first step toward increasing valency is to expose oneself to situations where one meets new people. Many singles say they are too "shy" or don't "want to invade somebody's privacy." We tell them that privacy is a cover-up word for a lonely person and shyness is only a fear that one's feelings will be unacceptable. We tell them that it is better to risk scaring off some supersensitive stranger than to pass up a potential intimate who doesn't know you exist— that if they really worry that their feelings may be unacceptable, they can use such feelings to break the ice:

"How do you feel about meeting me here like this? I feel ..."

In our pairing classes we teach introductory dialogue in three phases that will be explained more fully in later chapters:

1. *The role-free ice-breakers.* If a man meets a woman and she says, "What do you do?" a good response is, "I'd rather not tell you." Then, if she is sufficiently interested, she may say, "Are you trying to be mysterious?" A good reply is, "On the contrary, I want you to meet *me*, not my work." In this way, every "thing" is rejected for a here-and-now insight into thoughts and feelings.

2. *The authentic reservation.* We have found that intimacy is best served if a reservation about a

stranger is introduced as soon as possible. This may be considered presumptuous by the stranger, so it should be preceded by a request such as, "Would you mind if I share a feeling that keeps me from being friendly?" That opens the way to something like, "I've noticed that you mention your ex-husband every chance you get. That turns me off. Is there something about anything I've said that makes *you* uncomfortable?"

3. *Take advantage of any differences.* The exploration of polarities (see Chapter 12) can provide useful pairing material.

Everybody knows that some people are warmer and more open than others. But there are enormous numbers of potential intimates for everybody. One cannot predict their hair color, occupations, ages—any factor. But as potential intimates become realistic and valent, each step into a new room in which there are strangers becomes an adventurous exploration into a new country. They cannot know what they will find until they have actually walked the land, and not just dreamed about it. They must cross the rivers and feel the texture of the soil. Those who earnestly seek intimacy must become Darwins on an uncharted island, endlessly watchful, observant, curious, mapping.

Good sociological science supports this view. For people form a series of links with other people. You have a friend, who has a friend, who has a business acquaintance, who has a niece, who has a fellow club member, who has a lover, who has a neighbor, and so on. Each person with whom you spark intimacy is also a link in a chain. Once the chain is entered, one's world can enlarge enormously. Spotted along any of these chains are people who are likely to have strong pairing potential.

By becoming as highly valent as possible, people find many such chains opening up. It is good insurance for a good pairing when each partner maintains a fairly active, full social roster (nexus) of his own. Isolated exclusive pairings can generate paranoia and hostility against the outside world and become psychiatrically dangerous. Besides, the overlapping of two social circles provides stimulating grist for the conversational mill.

To keep running off to the woods (or the Bahamas) alone with a partner can kill a pairing. To have a social circle that recognizes the pairing as an entity, lends social sanction, and makes the relationship feel more real.

To build chains of social contacts, does not mean to become indiscriminate. It means to cultivate curiosity and interest. It means to explore and *then* discriminate on the solid basis of reality-tested information, not on the illusive basis of symbols, images, masks, or façades.

Many people are quite resistant to this view. One young man in a pairing class learned the techniques of intimacy well but used them only with chic, attractive women. He formed a number of relationships, but then he complained that they were unsatisfying, that the intimacy potential of these beauties was very limited for him.

Then one evening he came to class excitedly. "I know this will sound like a trite-as-hell testimonial," he said. "But I helped a little old lady today. She was struggling out the door of Saks loaded with packages, and I offered to help her and get her a cab. She said she had only three blocks to go, so I helped her all the way, and by the time we got there, we had quite a conversation going. She was meeting her granddaughter for cocktails, she said, and asked me to stay. What a granddaughter—superficially a little plain, maybe, but bright and warm and sensitive, and tomorrow we're—"

There are many, many such stories. The point is that the best way to find intimacy is to become an *intimate person*, open to the whole world of people, because that world is full of good pairing partners. Also, as one's experiences of creating intimacy multiply, people become more skilled as intimizers. When an experienced intimate finds a good pairing partner, he is better equipped to build a relationship, to elicit that potential partner's interest.

How does one choose people with whom to intimize? Proximity is one obvious way. The person in line with you, next to you at the lunch counter, waiting in the doctor's office with you—all are possibilities. You do, after all, need a little exposure-time with the person. Stopping someone rushing to an appointment would not be a good risk.

The chief criterion is your genuine interest in people generally—in some accident of their appearance, action, word, plight that catches your sympathetic attention. You can do much, however, to heighten your interest in others. The first device, is to take the trouble to look and really take note of the world and the people in it, as if you were a reporter who had to describe and explain them later. Sit near the door of a restaurant, and look closely at everyone who enters. Stand on a curb as the light changes, and take a good look at the people coming toward you. The very act of being interested will help give you an open look and outlook. Part of the pleasures of opening up a stranger is observing and being observed, and discovering what the observations mean.

Potential intimates are always interested in signs

that they are being accepted or excluded. Here are examples of gestures and sounds that may give some initial indication of whether a person is, at heart, open or closed.

Open-Receptive	*Closed-Exclusive*
feet crossed at the ankles. leaning against the wall, legs slightly apart, arms at the sides	legs crossed high and tight standing against the wall, one foot slightly forward, arms either crossed or raised (boxer stance)
palms out and open	clenched or clasped hands
face unobstructed, with eyes observing other people's faces	hands masking face, chin, or mouth, eyes on ceiling or down
reach and touch the other	scratch or pat self
purse or pipe held away from body	purse in lap, pipe in mouth
smacking lips or licking open mouth	tight lips, teeth clenched, rubbing nose
soft sigh, shoulders forward	sharp sigh with quick shoulder shrug
hands clasped b e h i n d head, armpits showing and chest protruding	one hand holds wrist down over genitals
direct, open look	shifting l o o k s, usually with hand on face ready to hide eyes
smoker letting ash build up on cigarette or cigar	constantly flicking ashes

Open-Receptive	*Closed-Exclusive*
drinker tends to put down glass or cup frequently	glass or cup held between self and others
smoker blowing smoke away from other person	creating a smokescreen between oneself and others

Research psychologists have emphasized supposedly significant sex differences in these gestures, but we have noticed an enormous overlap, the type of gesture depending more upon a person's degree of trust or mistrust than the sex of the person.

We recommend that gesture-readings, like mind-readings, should always be checked for accuracy. This can usually be done by direct sharing, such as: "I saw you leaning against the wall, not talking to anybody. I guess you'd just as soon leave this party—right?"

As you watch people, develop an eye for details that reveal special information. Are the clothes of foreign cut? Is there a special kind of pin in the lapel? What is the person carrying? What is he reading? Does he look often at his watch? Is he ordering the "diet special?" Is there any way of feeling what he feels right now? Is the light making it hard for him to read the menu? Does he loosen his collar because he is warm? Does this cough suggest much smoking? Does his easy joking with the waiter mean he feels expansive?

Many people are so self-concerned that they can be with a friend for an hour and not notice some fairly apparent physical discomfort, or his emotional uneasiness. This lack of awareness can seriously retard the growth of intimacy.

On the other hand, when one of our woman students began to use what we call the Intimate Eye, she came to class delighted with herself.

"I lunched with my boss twice, and both times I noticed that she did her chewing on one side of her mouth, and gingerly. I asked if a tooth bothered her. She said she could barely eat and had been miserable for weeks because of some dental work. She was intrigued by my noticing. She said she wished more people could get out of themselves. Then for the first time, she began to confide all sorts of inside, top-level information about the store."

In other words, the very expression of interest creates a responding interest in another person. (The unusual exception is what we call the Iceberg, the person who is determined to remain nonintimate. We warn students not to exhaust themselves trying to defrost an Iceberg, once a reasonable effort to create intimacy produces no response.)

The interest that one expresses must always be genuine, even if it is a little clumsy and self-conscious at first. This is the only way to overcome the suspicion that society assigns to an expressed interest in strangers.

(It is well to keep in mind that the aim of impactful encounter is not always a lasting intimacy. The pleasure of the process of discovery has value in itself.)

To illustrate the suspiciousness of strangers, we assigned students to stand, one at a time, at one end of a long, narrow construction walkway on a Beverly Hills street. As soon as someone entered the walkway from the other end, the student would set out toward him, focusing on the stranger from the distance, observing him closely and not yielding the way easily.

So conditioned are people not to look at strangers, that the reactions were remarkable. Always, the stranger became a little troubled. Some males reacted as if the students, male or female, were challenging them to combat. They became tense and pugnacious. Others were self-conscious, inspecting themselves to see what was wrong with them. The vast majority acted as if the students wanted something from them. A few made such remarks to the students as, "Are you lost?" "Need directions?" "What did you say?" Two told the students what time it was—actually illuding themselves that they had heard a question asked of them.

Expressed interest of any sort, then, carries great impact. But that impact can turn into acute anxiety and withdrawal unless it is promptly and logically accounted for. For example, telling someone at a meeting, "I was interested in what you said about the problem," is convincing. But the interest must be real and shown by specific comments that prove the genuineness.

Most people are perceptive enough to sense phoniness. When they do, they need only halt the manipulator, level with him by open confrontation and flush out his ulterior motives. We urge pairers not to collude with manipulators by being polite. Since manipulators exploit good manners, they do not deserve to profit by them.

Sharing objects is not the highest-impact approach, but it is reasonably effective. Petting someone's dog is a fairly common example. But you had better really like the dog or *he* may sense the sham. In general, if the interest one expresses and attempts to share is real, its reality will convey itself.

The shared-object approach works best when it makes a reference to one's own personality and makes some statement about one's own style or concerns. Another of our training exercises is to imagine that there is only a short airplane ride in which to make contact with someone and to begin an intimacy that could be continued. We use as a model the Los Angeles-San Francisco run, which lasts about forty-five minutes.

The week she heard about this exercise, one of our students, an imaginative and honest woman, actually found herself on this trip, seated next to a very attractive man. He was engrossed in a copy of *Playboy*, reading a long article. Ten minutes went by, and she could think of no real way to express interest in the man himself, except to say that she found him attractive. The idea of doing this made her very uncomfortable.

Our rule for identifying and maximizing real interest is: meditate. Our student gave herself one full minute to concentrate hard on the man beside her, straining all her ability to observe and gain information. But she kept being caught up by the magazine, involuntarily reading along with him. It distracted her from meditating. "Finally," she reported to us, "it occurred to me that this was my strongest point of mutual interest. I was afraid of sounding ridiculous, but I mustered my courage and said, 'When you get to the nude in the centerfold, would you mind showing it to me?' "

The man was a little startled, but, staring at her, he turned at once, a little uncomfortably, to the picture. They looked at it together, in silence. And then he asked, "Do you mind telling me why you wanted to see this?"

"Well, I like to look at nude photographs," she said. "The human body is always fascinating to me."

Then she meditated for just a moment and expressed the feeling that popped into her mind. "For some reason," she added, "I felt I could ask you, and you wouldn't mind. You look very poised, very adult."

The dialogue was at once off and running. The "intimate eye" had seen her own interest and his potential. She revealed her accessibility as a responsible human being who was willing to risk his rejection and felt attracted enough to take the gamble. Her "style" was real in the best classic sense; she was honestly curious—not "handing him a line"—and he responsed with delight.

We suggest that students try meditating at greater length and alone before doing some of our exercises. This sounds strange to Western ears. But we recommend meditation to achieve reality, rather than transcend it, to dissolve traffic jams in one's head and to clarify for oneself what options are available to solve a problem and to decide which is the best choice.

The self-hypnotic focus of meditation that shuts out distractions can be any object that creates monotonous patterns of sight or sound—a mobile, a flame, a clock pendulum, ocean waves, gentle flowing water, sunsets, sunrises. You watch, concentrate, relax, and meditate.

You may wish to phone someone, but you are reluctant because you know the other has expressed a desire for distance. Is your instinct to re-establish communication at this time what you really want to do in this relationship? Are you indulging your sense of insecurity or expressing your sense of caring?

Engage yourself in dialogue, perhaps even out loud, expressing both sides of the situation—your conflicting feelings—as fully as you can. If you have a tape recorder, you can even record your "inner dialogue." When you are through, play it back. Feedback is useful in hearing yourself. Listen carefully to your dialogue, and determine which action is most realistic for you.

You will know what feels right and what feels wrong. If you are still ambivalent, practice some more meditation or talk over your quandary with your partner or a friend.

To use valency to best advantage in the search for potential intimates, we advise students to show unashamed curiosity toward almost anyone of the opposite sex who passes what ought to be an easy test of attractiveness. Appearances can leave dreadfully false cues, because in Western culture they reflect the pressures of conformity far more than they mirror personality.

The ways to show curiosity are:

1. Avoid the "closed-exclusive" stances, look carefully and directly, and show that you are interested in the stranger's conversation.
2. Don't categorize (such as married or not married, educated or not educated, fun or no fun). The surface or the mood of the moment can be deceptive indeed.
3. When meeting a stranger in a crowd it is important to isolate him or her, for in the very beginning it is true that "two is company and three is a crowd." Sometimes the simple act of taking a person aside is all that is needed to begin a potentially intimate involvement.

There are efficient and inefficient ways to obtain the feel for the intimacy potential of a stranger. Most people use indirect (fishing trip) gropings to discover it; we recommend direct (cutting bait) methods. Here are two strangers anywhere:

THE FISHING TRIP WAY (traditional)	THE CUTTING BAIT WAY (Leveling)
SHE: Oh, what's that button in your lapel?	I'd like to know you.
HE: It's my Chamber of Commerce button.	I'm glad. I noticed you too.
SHE: Where's that? I'm from Texas myself.	I hoped you would.
HE: That's the Arizona coat of arms. Have you seen it before?	Let's sit over there where we can chat.
SHE: No, but I've been all through Arizona.	Yes, I'd like that.

Basically, the pairer has only one question when meeting an interesting stranger: how to display interest.

A young woman waiting at the airport for her brother to arrive notices an attractive man nervously pacing up and down:

SHE:
I noticed you pacing up and down while I've been sitting here.

HE:
Waiting makes me nervous.

SHE:
Whom are you waiting for? I'm waiting for my brother. (She is not just interviewing him, but modeling the way she'd like him to respond.)

HE:
It's a business associate.

SHE (relieved):
I'd like to talk to you some more but you make me nervous with your pacing.

HE (laughs):
Well, I don't want to do that. Do you have time for a cup of coffee?

The only danger of the direct approach is that it may scare many strangers off. To insure against this, we caution pairing students to be prepared for a puzzled reaction but then to take advantage of the puzzlement by openly discussing it.

Tact tells people that there are limits to directness, and that when they are exceeded, alienation is likely to result rather quickly. This sort of tactlessness is exemplified by sexual invitations made before any intimate exchange has taken place. For the person so invited feels certain that he or she is being thinged in a highly exploitative way, and resistance zooms.

The best example is that of the brash and leering male who winks and makes suggestive remarks to women he has scarcely met. When he does this or, worse still, touches, he is almost guaranteeing his rejection. In fact, he usually knows that he is making any relationship impossible. This allows him to make a public display of his questionable "masculine" sex aggression and daring, without ever having to follow through. In most cases, he is acting out a hostility to women. Almost any salesgirl, receptionist, or airline stewardess who is trapped into putting up with him, and has to keep smiling, senses his hostility and hates him for it.

Many women follow the same pitiful pattern. They make a display of suggestiveness, brushing against uncomfortably trapped men, winking, making pseudoseductive remarks. A few very blind males may be flattered and turned on. The majority know they are being treated as objects, for ego-gratification, and they withdraw.

When they have met, potential pairers can increase mutual interest in each others' real selves by such simple devices as drawing self-portraits. A cocktail napkin will do. Artistic quality is irrelevant. If both make drawings simultaneously, this communication exercise works better because it eliminates kibitzing. The point is to reduce the chance of wasting an opportunity with impersonal trivia.

This is self-presentation and calls for no amateur analysis of the other. It is good pairing technique to explain to the partner what your self-portrait means to you, and you can say anything you like. If you have drawn a head, you might try, "When I'm with you, I'm all head and intellectually stimulated." Or, "My best part is my face." If you have drawn a complete body, you could say, "With you I feel free enough to show off my figure."

If he draws his portrait and asks you what it means, the good pairer's response is, "You tell me; it's a *self*-portrait!"

9

The
art of
impacting

MOST people are intuitively aware of the need to have impact on another in order to begin an intimate relationship. But their conventional methods are generally quite ineffective. The inability to impact on a partner is one of the most disastrous failures of pairing. We hear the results of these failures constantly in the familiar, bitter lament: "He (or she) doesn't even know I'm alive!"

In courting-style affairs or marriages, impacting can become almost impossible and its lack produces a lackluster dissatisfaction that is intimacy-killing. The failure to "get a rise" out of a partner, the frustration of just hearing him say "Yes, dear" and little more, becomes a prime cause of unfaithfulness. Sooner or later there usually begins a hunt for a more responsive impact target, as one or both partners act out their desperate hunger to have a powerful effect on some other.

The no-impact state is often the result of the false take-me-as-I-am ideology. Many people rationalize,

"If you loved me, you wouldn't ask me to change in any way; you would not try to have impact on me." For a change of some kind in a partner is the only way impact is shown: an affectionate turn-on, perhaps, or the breaking of an annoying habit. The deliberate creation of a no-change, no-impact state in a pairing is probably the most effective way to bring it to an end.

And even if the traditional courting ways of impacting do start a relationship moving, they also plant troublesome seeds of dissatisfaction.

It is worth taking a closer look at some of the more common impacting techniques, to see why they are usually doomed to failure or create only a tenuous bond without generating intimacy. Often, if the partners succeed, it is only because they are interested enough at the start to want to succeed.

Curt and Joyce have seen one another four or five times at PTA meetings. They have been introduced and are both attracted, but they have had no chance to talk. Curt knows that Joyce has a little girl in the school and no husband. Joyce knows that Curt has two youngsters, and no wife. Beyond that, they have little knowledge about each other.

Curt has contrived several times to be with Joyce at the coffee-and-cake break after the meeting, but he does not know that Joyce maneuvered just as diligently to make this possible. At the moment they are largely attractive things to one another. Their attempts to reach each other have been cut off by their personal attractiveness. As soon as the PTA lets out, Joyce has at least one man at her elbow, and as Curt moves toward her, some lady invariably bars his path with a question, usually concerning his role as county District Attorney.

But tonight they have been lucky. They sat beside

one another through the meeting and are now headed for the refreshment table, free to talk. To see the effect that each intends and compare it with the effect actually produced, the conversation is presented as a quadrilog.

THEY SAY	THEY THINK
CURT: You certainly look great tonight, hair all done up and everything.	*She always looks so turned out. Must get good alimony.*
JOYCE: Thank you, sir. I had it done for an appointment tomorrow.	*I did it myself, and for you. It took me nearly two hours.*
I might say that you're your usual bandbox self. Such a nice jacket.	*These swinging bachelors can afford to dress up even for PTA.*
CURT: Thanks. it's my favorite. I bought it to go with my car, my pride and joy.	*Damn. She's clothes conscious, too.*
JOYCE: Oh? What kind of car?	*It has to be a sports car.*
CURT: Little Panther roadster.	*That should give me a few points.*
JOYCE: I seem to remember riding in one last summer when I was in France.	*You don't have to know that my in-laws got me the tickets.*
CURT: Wish I could get away more, but with my job, there's always something.	*I knew she was the jet-set type. I'd better change the subject.*

THEY SAY	THEY THINK
JOYCE: Oh? What do you do?	*I don't want you to know I asked around about you. I'll bet he's always at big political meetings, and things.*
CURT: (lightly.) District Attorney. Benton County's own crusader.	
JOYCE: My great uncle was a district attorney —of Chicago.	*So I never met him, and he was only my grandmother's half brother.*
CURT: Oh, gosh. Henry's over there, waving at me. See? The telephone. It never fails. Every time I get anywhere near a pretty girl, someone murders someone or blows up a bank. Will you excuse me? I hope I won't have to go downtown.	*I should have known. Money, travel, and now old family. And with her looks, the competition must be tough. It looks pretty hopeless, anyway. She seems out of my league.*
JOYCE: Of course. You have to look after the county, after all.	*Anyway, its probably hopeless. What would he see in me?*

Curt does have to go downtown, and weeks pass before they talk again. They have made a poor start. They have both concentrated on imaging as a way of achieving impact, shutting out intimacy. They have felt each other out, like boxers, keeping their real feelings secret.

Both had eagerly sought time together and carefully prepared for it. Then they used it for negative effect and parted with a sense of insecurity and hopelessness.

Neither has conveyed his interest and attraction, and both have gathered false impressions of one another. Curt assumes Joyce has too much money and social position for him. He imagines her as a well-alimonied divorcee. He does not know that she was widowed when her naval-officer husband was killed in Vietnam. He certainly could not guess that she feels a little overawed by his political position, that she thinks of him as the spoiled bachelor, rather than a lonely, overworked man who was deserted by an alcoholic wife, and who now scratches for time to spend looking after his children.

Later, both enrolled in one of our pairing classes and Curt chose Joyce to practice an introduction exercise that we use, a ritual that violates nearly all the traditional rules of introducing—and succeeds marvelously.

Obviously, both needed some coaching in how to achieve true impact. Because we insist that good pairing conversations must always be open and honest, their dialog suffices to tell the story; for what is said in such a conversation is also essentially what is felt.

For these classes, a large, comfortable room is used. The students are seated in individual uphol-stered chairs on casters, so that they can easily move into whatever positions of distance or closeness are comfortable for them. Curt draws his chair to within five feet of Joyce. She does not retreat; without seeming to notice what she is doing, she even draws her chair a little closer still.

Such physical distancing can serve as a clue to the pairer. If he begins a contact from a few feet away, he may observe whether his partner comes closer or withdraws, which often indicates the degree of the other's interest. By leaving some distance at the start, he gives his partner a chance to express this interest, and also to express her general feelings about just how close she wants to be to people. Many students are not too comfortable at very close range, especially with strangers, and when the situation is laden with anxiety.

CURT (to the coach):
This is just an introduction ritual, is that it? Just making yourself known to the other person?

COACH:
Don't say "just." You are trying to have some real impact from the very first moment of encounter.

CURT:
Okay. Joyce, my name is Curt Burroughs. and I'm the District Attorney of Benton County, and I have some questions I'd like to ask you, ma'am. (The group chuckles.)

COACH:
Whoa, Curt. That was clever. But cleverness is not very important, unless that's what you want to impact with, rather than your total person. You'll be better off if your subjective feelings have impact. Who you are, and what role you play in society, are not very important here. Even your real name is not very important. You want to present your *self*. Let me try a little demonstration to show you how much strangers can find out about each other without knowing their real names. Please introduce yourselves, not with your real names, but with a nickname that feels right at this moment. After all, nobody gets to choose his first name, so these

names don't usually tell much about a person. Take an animal name if you like, a flower, a state of feeling. Now meditate on this for a minute. You need some thoughtful focus to become aware of your own feelings, before you display them to others.

CURT (after meditating):
My name is Jason.

COACH:
Now explain what state of feeling is communicated by that name.

CURT (grinning):
I was thinking of the mythical Jason, and I feel as if I'm going adventuring, treasure-hunting.

JOYCE:
That's what I thought you meant. And as soon as you said that, I had my name. I almost called myself Fleece, but that would be awful. Fluff is silly, I guess. But it's what came into my mind. (She reddens a little.) It's the closest I could come. (She and Curt smile at one another, delighted to discover the obvious meaning of the names.)

COACH:
Now, you see, you've had impact on one another. When you meet someone, you might try to explain the naming exercise, as I did, and say that you've learned this new way of getting acquainted and would like to test it out. Try to stop other people before they can give their true names. Ask them to name you, and you can name them. It gives you insights about the relationship, and sets a pattern of openness. Now go ahead, Curt.

CURT:
Well—do you live in this part of town?

COACH:

I'll have to stop you again, Curt. Don't interview her. You won't be able to elicit intimacy with geography. That's again avoiding the goal of having impact. Begin by expressing a *feeling*; then you'll really bring out a feeling response from your partner. Think. Meditate, and don't be glib.

CURT:

I guess the strongest feeling I have right now is that I'm glad of this excuse to talk to you, Joyce, and I'm—a little nervous about it, too.

JOYCE:

Why should you be nervous?

CURT:

Well, I've been feeling so attracted to you at the PTA, and ...

COACH:

That's the general idea, Curt. But I'll interrupt because we've learned that maximum impact comes from sticking to the here-and-now. Your feelings this minute are what carry the most impact, not your historical feelings. You are trying to create a feeling of immediacy and open intensity, which in turn will make Joyce want to trust you and share your feelings with you.

CURT (smiling):

I'm certainly just as attracted now, Joyce, as I was at the PTA. And I'm nervous, because I'm afraid I won't really be able to get to you. (There is a long pause. Then he turns to the coach.) Can't I just make conversation? That's what I'd normally do.

COACH:

All right, Curt. Why don't you turn to me for a

minute, and we'll have a huddle on your strategy. Let's look at some of your options. (Joyce turns away, as if respecting Curt's privacy.) Don't turn away, Joyce. This isn't a secret huddle. Everything here is out in the open. You are not the enemy or the competition. And we are not scheming in any way to trick or even surprise you. Pairing is an open interaction, not a con game. It's not the sort of manipulating game that Eric Berne described in *Games People Play*. Now, Curt, you can, of course, just make conversation. But that will have low impact. It will also be slow. Joyce may have to catch a plane any minute, for all you know. You are trying to reveal yourself in this conversation, to be open. How shall we get you to reach into yourself?

One obvious thing is to tell Joyce what about her attracts you, specifically and genuinely. That's good. But if you leave it at that alone, it may not elicit much genuine response unless you also tell her how you are affected by the way she is behaving at this moment. That is dynamic. It affirms the reality of her behavior toward you, and perhaps makes her more aware of feelings of her own that are now unconscious. Another possibility, which is also dynamic, is to tell her how you feel about the way she responds to what you say—for example, in the naming exercise. Or you could tell her what you hope is going to result from this exchange between the two of you. That would get her to consider future possibilities of relating to you, and open up some new possibilities of talking about what you would need to do to get her to fulfill that hope. Now with these things in mind, meditate again.

CURT (he thinks hard):
It's hard to say exactly why you attract me, Joyce.

But it may be the way a beautiful and striking woman like you is really a little shy, not brash or cocky at all. I like the way you drop your glance and almost blush when you catch me staring at you. See what I mean? You're starting to do it right now.

COACH:
That's a good start, Curt. By verbalizing her reaction to you, you bring her into the exchange. You are making her more aware of the feelings that produce these reactions. This makes your relationship more real. Also, when you are keenly observant of the detail of another person's habits or behavior, that has great impact. It turns you into a person who recognizes them, who really gives attention to their existence, on a person level. That means that you think of them as important.

CURT (nods his understanding):
Now what?

COACH:
Well, you've observed a reaction and you've commented on it. Now you want to encourage her to express her feelings a little, as a way of involving her. What do you think her behavior might mean, for example?

CURT:
I guess maybe it means—I hope it means that maybe you're a little curious about me, Joyce.

COACH:
Good. Now check out this conclusion of yours, so you'll know how true it is.

CURT:
Is it true? Are you a little shy because you're curious about me?

JOYCE:

Well, yes. Yes I am, a little. I've noticed you staring at me, and I wonder why. Of course (she smiles), you drop your eyes, too, whenever I catch you looking at me.

COACH:

That's fine, Joyce. But I think perhaps you could have made a little objection that Curt was mind-reading you. Since we can't tell what people are thinking or feeling unless they tell us, we have to be very tactful when we guess about them. We should ask permission to make the guess, in order to be sure the guess does not cause a turn-off by its invasiveness. It's like walking into someone's home without knocking.

Okay, Joyce, now you have some options you can follow up. If you wonder about why he stares, you can ask him to be more explicit. The same is true if you wonder about his dropping his eyes when you catch him.

In any case, you have a relationship now, though it's just a small one. But it *is* personal. It is specific to the two of you and sets itself apart. You have a basis for relating, and that should be deepened.

CURT:

You mean, now I should tell her more about myself —name, occupation, and so on?

COACH:

Well, if those details fit in, they are harmless once you've made impact. They may help involve the other person. But such things usually have little to do with creating any kind of bond or deepening the involvement. Surprisingly, you can reach the next level of intimacy best by introducing a *reserva-*

tion about Joyce as soon as you can, something real but *negative*. It should be a doubt you have about the relationship, based on a first impression of some actual word, act, or other clue that you perceive. Remember, your doubts and fears should be truly felt and openly displayed. You are sharing your feelings. You are not trying to manipulate another person. For instance, you might feel, and say, "You're moving in on me too fast. I feel overpowered and want to protect myself from your invasion. I don't like feeling overpowered. I'd like to go on with you, but please slow down."

CURT:

I suppose the biggest reservation I have about approaching you, Joyce, is that I'm a little afraid you may be out of my league. I've seen other men crowd around you, and I know that the competition is heavy. I've heard you mention traveling abroad and the like, and your clothes look expensive. So I know you're busy all the time. and anyway, on a city salary, it would be hard for me to keep up with the expensive dates you're used to. You'd think I was pretty small time.

COACH:

Time out, Curt. Your reservations are good ones, and they're obviously genuine. But you're making a lot of assumptions about Joyce. You are reading her mind again, without checking it out.

CURT:

Not really. Look at her clothes, for example.

COACH:

Yes, she does dress very well. But still, we must not invade people's minds and make assumptions. Her father may be in the dress business. We also call

130

that *mind-raping*, ascribing thoughts and feelings to someone else without checking them out. It not only creates illusions in our own minds, and false reasoning, but the person to whom we do it is bound to feel alienated. He or she feels we are misreading them. And they are likely to resent the lack of understanding, as well as the invasion.

CURT:

You mean I shouldn't guess what's going on in Joyce's mind?

COACH:

Well, of course you can guess, or reason. But then you should immediately check this out against reality by asking a question. And if you want to say what you *think* she is thinking, then you should ask her permission. In fact, we recommend that you always play safe by asking a person's permission before making any inroads into his privacy—even before making any negative statement such as a reservation. Would you like to try stating your reservations again?

CURT:

Okay. Joyce, may I give you a reservation I have about you, and about us?

JOYCE:

Yes, you may.

CURT:

Well, I'm afraid you may be out of my league. I suspect you have too much money or social position. It's partly the things you've said about places you've been, and it's partly the well-dressed, sophisticated look you have, the way you have your hair done, that sort of thing. I'm afraid I'd be dull for you.

JOYCE (to the coach):
Is there anything special I'm supposed to do now?

COACH:
There are some things you might do to have greater impact on Curt, or to make for faster, better communication. But why don't you just react naturally, genuinely?

JOYCE:
All right. (Turns to Curt.) I'm very flattered. You see, the truth is, I'm sort of scraping along. I don't go out much. But I love to sew, and I put a lot of time into my clothes. And thank you for what you said about my hair. I can't afford the beauty parlor regularly. So I spent hours putting it up and combing it out today.

CURT:
Still, you seem to have been around a lot, and you must be very popular with men. I just went to a country law school and then got a job in the D.A.'s office.

JOYCE:
I never finished the country college I went to. I married my husband instead. He was a Navy pilot, and I lost him in Vietnam.

COACH:
You see, Curt, how much information you got by being genuine about your feelings toward Joyce? You're good with words. But suppose you'd gone on your assumptions about Joyce. and tried to seem clever and debonair. How do you suppose she would have reacted?

CURT:
I suppose—wait a minute. I'll ask her.

COACH:

Now you're getting the idea.

CURT: (to Joyce):

How about it? Suppose I'd tried to show you that I was pretty sophisticated—made my job sound good, dropped the names of politicians I meet, mentioned my sports car, which is my one extravagance—that's what I probably would have done before this class. What would you have said?

JOYCE:

Suppose I answer that by giving you *my* reservation about *you?* (To the coach)Is that all right?

COACH:

It's perfect. Curt's next step would have been to ask you for your reservations. This gives him a chance to understand more about how you see him. And it continues to involve both of you in more real discussion, more of the realities of the pair. Go ahead, Joyce.

JOYCE:

The truth is, Curt, I overheard you telling someone at one of the PTA meetings that you almost didn't make it because you had an emergency meeting at the Mayor's house with some State officials, and I was impressed. I'd known what your job was, because you mentioned it the first time we ever talked. And now, though I was interested in you, I thought to myself, what could he possibly see in a dull housewife with kids? I might get taken to some official function and use the wrong fork or something. Besides, you're nice looking and have a good job, and you're free—the perfect-catch type. You can have your pick, and you must be in demand to fill in at parties and things all the time, and—

COACH:
Hold it, Joyce, You're starting to make assumptions. Try to rephrase what you said at the last so that you present your observations of Curt as hypotheses, hunches that are subject to revision or reservations by him.

JOYCE:
Well, you're nice looking, and I guess you're free, aren't you? I mean, this is a singles group.

CURT:
I'm not married, but I've got two children, and they take practically all the spare time I can get. And what with paying for housekeeping and baby-sitting and alimony, there's not much left over to be a swinger with. But are you saying (he grins) that *you* were afraid you couldn't interest *me?*

JOYCE:
(She nods.)

CURT:
I'll be darned. But what if I'd tried to be clever and impressive? You were going to tell me how you'd have reacted to that.

JOYCE:
I guess I'd have dropped a lot of things about France, and avoided explaining that my husband was stationed there for two years, and we lived on the base. I'd have tried to make myself look sophisticated.

CURT:
Which is exactly what was worrying me. (He shakes his head.) I think that would have stopped me; it would have made you look that much more out of my league.

JOYCE:
And I would have been completely discouraged if you'd made my fantasy about *you* look any more real.

CURT:
We would have been finished before we started—and for no real reason.

COACH:
There are more steps in our "Instant Intimacy" introduction, beyond the impact expression of feelings and the exchange of reservations. But tell me, Joyce, how has this experience affected you so far?

JOYCE:
I guess mainly, Curt has become real to me. It's hard to express, but it's as if he had been a kind of cardboard character for me, and now he has three dimensions.

CURT:
I know what you mean. You're a lot more human to me, too. It's like the difference between seeing a very good photograph and meeting the person himself. You get a very different impression.

COACH:
I think you'll all find that this is exactly what happens. By this method you get the feeling of really meeting a person. You get a sense of genuineness, of warmth. And the illusions, and the best-foot-forward images, are broken.

It is worth interrupting this conversation to review what has happened in this exercise. The details of name, address, status, work, and the like have been played down. This is *imaging* and sometimes hard to resist. People such as Curt are aware that certain attributes evoke automatic interest and approval. The doctor, priest, and judge, for example, know that their labels give them a certain "good guy" status, and a certain appearance of power. Wealthy people with old family names need only say these names to achieve some impact.

Some people use their activities to make other people's ears perk up. Lines such as, "When I was having breakfast in Rome this morning," will draw attention, as will, "At the opera opening last night —." Other people toss off attributes that convey no special quality but do evoke curiosity. They could be anything from, "I was born as a quadruplet," to "My first name is the same as my last, James James."

These impacting devices appear to work dependably. They resemble the sure-fire joke one always tells at parties. But their effect is usually just to "thing" oneself.

Life today is hurried. Encounters are brief. People tend to develop television minds, accustomed to quick, shallow exposures. Their attention span grows shorter. When one presents oneself as a symbol or thing, one actually slows the process of relating. For having identified oneself in this way, one must break through not only natural uneasiness and resistance to reach reality, but also the façade one has now implanted in the mind of the other (name-dropper, gag man, etc.).

Introductory approaches that are contrived through little shams—from asking the girl on the beach what time it is to dropping one's handkerchief—tend merely to put people on guard. The objects of one's attention are likely to become preoccupied with questioning the genuineness of the device, or even become offended by the apparent trickery. Feelings of suspicion for the stranger are enhanced.

That is why the most effective approach to intimacy is the expression of real feelings in a real way. It also is the surest way to evoke trust enough to elicit the real feelings of the other.

Efficiency is not the only reason why these feelings should be expressed as soon as possible. Trust-building is most usefully applied before imaging or symbolizing or seductive manipulating creates a feeling of mistrust. With immediate impact, both partners become genuinely involved before rejection fears lead them to create troublesome illusions in their own and one another's minds. The need for illusive imaging to win approval of the other is sharply reduced, for in expressing real feelings to someone, one also expresses trust and acceptance.

This potential for basic trust, acceptance, and intimacy exists between almost any two human beings. For virtually everyone has the potential for some degree of intimate exchange. Loneliness, fear, joy, and many other feelings are so universal that they can be shared with anyone—at least in some small but mutually gratifying way.

So anyone who can be open and genuine, can approach anyone else with a probability of some success. This probability frees people to explore the potentials of any number of relationships. For in a philosophic as well as a psychological sense, all human beings live in the same village and can greet each other as neighbors.

10

Rejection
without
fear

DOES all this alarm our pairing students? Indeed it does. When they are asked to challenge their fears of making fresh human contacts, many feel sick to their stomachs, get dizzy, have headaches or an urge to urinate. We have even seen a few desperate souls faint.

When approached by others, some people are overcome by the primitive urge of wanting to run away in the hope of being chased. Other body emergency responses are paleness, as the blood rushes to skeletal muscles; deep breathing in preparation for flight; tensed body ready for quick flight.

Plainly, such reactions are somewhat exaggerated, although they become understandable in the light of the overmobilization theory. Yet they are real, and must be dealt with. That is why we developed rejection exercises.

We ask a student to select another of the opposite sex. One of the pair becomes the approacher, and the other is the rejector. Later, we reverse the rolls, so that each undergoes the experiences of rejecting as well as being rejected; the purpose is to learn that neither role produces really unbearable distress. Readers might like to eavesdrop on such an exercise, and should be able to do it themselves.

The pair are first instructed to meditate for a minute on their own feelings of attraction or resistance toward each other. Very often, in such concentration, we suggest that they close their eyes.

They are told that whatever wishes they express must be real and authentic. If the person who is going to do the rejecting begins to feel that he really wants to accept, he must do so. If the person who is approaching loses interest, he must stop.

Usually, we begin with the woman approaching, to help break down the stereotypes that still hamper the female sex. Valerie has selected Glen to reject her. She is told by coach:

"Meditate on what you really like in Glen and what you want to get from him. Tell him of your wishes and attraction for him. Then be ready for his response. If he rejects your approach as "too much-too soon," slow down. Ask him what he *could* give you. Then see if you can compromise and accept what you can get."

A coach, either a trained instructor, or an experienced student who is very familiar with our methods, stands by to correct errors and offer assistance when needed. The reader might pay particular attention to the principles brought out by the coach. For these principles recur through all aspects of the pairing system.

Valerie is an attractive, well-groomed divorcee of about forty-five. Glen, thirty-five, has never been married. He is a shy, quiet man of average looks, who has a great fear of displeasing others. It is hard for him to say no.

VALERIE (nervously moistening her lips):
Well, I feel foolish doing this, Glen, and of course, I know that you're a lot younger than I am, and—

COACH (interrupting):
Stop! What does age have to do with this? Are you proposing marriage? (Valerie shakes her head.) Are you thinking of something you would really like to have from Glen? (Valerie nods.) Then simply tell him what you want. Tell him your real feelings. I get the impression that you may be setting up the situation in advance so you can explain a possible rejection later on.

VALERIE:
Well, honestly, I feel ridiculous enough doing this. A woman just doesn't ask a man for a date in any real circumstance, and after all, it is true that Glen is years younger than I am.

COACH:
You are a woman asking a man for a date only if that's what you have in mind. Remember, it's up to you to choose what you ask for. You should have meditated and concentrated on that wish. Focus on it and summon up a lot of strong feeling for it. But don't expect to get what you want if you don't ask.

VALERIE:
It's just that what we do here, it seems to me, isn't what gets done in society. A woman doesn't ask—

COACH:
In our past courtship etiquette, no, she doesn't. But that etiquette is changing. And remember, we are

aiming at reaching intimacy. When a woman does ask for what she wants, she gets attention and interest. You're expressing your real feelings, after all. And when someone does that, the genuineness shows through, and is very persuasive. The risk is not really great.

VALERIE:

Well, all right. (She sighs.) Glen, I've been watching you here in the group. You don't say a great deal, but what you do say comes out with so much sincerity. And I can see you're a gentle person. You know, I get so tired of this Lothario game that most men play. They all want to act like movie stars and try to seduce you, just to fatten up their egos.

COACH:

Cut it out, Valerie. Don't you think just as many women play Sex Queen? And if you don't think women seduce as an ego trip, you just haven't been looking. Remember, Glen is a man. So don't attack his group in that unfair way.

VALERIE:

Sorry. It's just the way I see it, I guess. Glen, it's very simple. I—I just think you'd be a nice person to spend a Sunday with, talking and doing simple things.

GLEN (a little tritely):

Well, I've watched you, too, Valerie, and I think you're interesting. And of course, I'd like to spend some time talking with you—but—but—

COACH:
Glen, are these your real feelings? Are they very, very genuine?

GLEN:
More or less. After all, you can't be rude, can you? I really wouldn't want to hurt Valerie, certainly not over some game.

COACH:
But this isn't a game. Its whole purpose is to be completely real. If you make a commitment, it's a real one here. Now, of course, we want to be tactful. But you sound as if you're not really going to resist Valerie, as if you are about to accommodate by saying yes to everything. Am I wrong about that?

GLEN:
I'm just starting out to be polite, that's all. Can I say I'm not interested? (The coach nods.) I don't think I can do that. (The coach smiles. Glen sighs heavily.) Okay. Look, Valerie, I think you're a very attractive woman, with a very good figure. But to be honest, you've been just another member of the group to me. I mean, I'm sympathetic to the things you're saying. But I don't feel any bond at all between us. Mostly, you're talking about men taking advantage of you, and polite conventions. Well, it's all sort of—uninteresting. It doesn't sound too real.

VALERIE (looking defeated):
I guess that's that.

COACH:
You're not going to quit, are you? Glen's just given you a clue. He says you cover up what you feel, so

143

that you're not a whole personality to him. That's why we urge you to expose more of your real feelings. It's the best way to get another person's attention. Besides, you really haven't even told Glen what your full wish is.

VALERIE:

Well, I'll start over. Glen, what I said about being interested in you as a person is real. I work hard at my job, and I often work Saturdays. So I like to have some relaxation and companionship on Sunday. I have in mind to pack a really nice picnic lunch for us—I love to cook, and I make the best roasted chicken with a special stuffing—and take it to the zoo in the park with a bottle of good wine and my homemade spice cake. I'd love to spend Saturday night cooking for us.

GLEN:

That does sound good, the picnic thing. But on Sunday, I usually see my mother.

VALERIE:

You could see her in the morning, couldn't you?

GLEN:

If I do, I go to church with her. Then she fixes lunch for me. It's sort of a ritual.

VALERIE:

I'm afraid that maybe the idea really doesn't appeal to you, Glen, and—

COACH:

Valerie, you've just violated two of our most basic rules of pairing. First, you were mind-reading Glen. You were making assumptions about another person's thoughts. That we don't do. How can you know what Glen is thinking unless he tells you? If you don't check out your assumptions, you're bound to behave according to your own illusions, not according to the facts.

Secondly, you went out of your way to suggest a negative outcome to Glen. That's against your own interest. You want to keep Glen's interest alive as long as possible, not help him to let it die.

VALERIE:

All right. (Inhales again.) Does the idea have any appeal to you at all, Glen? I mean, really?

GLEN:

Well, yes, it does—if I can just find some way not to disappoint my mother. I mean, she really is alone, and I feel Sunday is the one day when I can do something with her. But by the time three o'clock comes, I'm very glad to go.

VALERIE:

I guess Sunday is out. (Then she brightens a little.) Unless you'd like to go straight from your mother's to the zoo, and we could make it a picnic supper afterward?

GLEN:

Mother lives twenty miles from the zoo. And you know how the Sunday traffic is.

VALERIE:

Oh. (She settles back.)

COACH:

Valerie, it sounds to me as if Glen is not really saying no to the supper.

VALERIE (to Glen):

You mean that you would be able to have supper with me?

GLEN (uncomfortable now):
Well—Yes, I guess—

COACH:
Glen, are you really mobilizing all your resistance?
Are you bringing up all your reluctances?

GLEN:
More or less. After all, you agreed that I should be
tactful.

COACH:
Tactful, yes. But not falsely accommodating. You
must not agree out of a feeling of obligation. If you
do, you will only be uncomfortable and resentful in
the long run. Do you still have some honest reservations that make you want to say no, down deep?

GLEN (speaking to Valerie):
Really, it does seem like a nice idea. But—you see,
well, you *are* older than I am, and frankly, the truth
is that I'd be a little embarrassed if people saw me
on a date with you. It's my fault. I'm just very easily
embarrassed.

VALERIE (she is somewhat crushed):
In that case—

COACH:
Wait, Valerie: You know you're older. You
brought it up, didn't you? So listen carefully to
what Glen says. He'd like to have supper with you.
The age difference bothers him because you're going to be seen together in public.

VALERIE:
Oh, this is ridiculous. I don't have to crawl to get a
man. You people have absurd ideas. If a man wants

to see a woman, he can do the asking. This isn't right.

COACH:
That's a convenient way to end your discomfort, of course. But think about it a minute. You have been reminded that your age really does make a difference. Yet at least you really know Glen's feelings. Without coaching, he would have agreed to the picnic out of politeness and out of embarrassment at rejecting you. Then on Sunday he would have been uncomfortable and resentful, and the supper would have been a disaster. That is why, in pairing, if we have any doubts, we check them out by asking directly. Now, I think you can see that Glen really might like to have supper with you, and you can have contact with him, as you said you wanted—

VALERIE:
Is that true, Glen? (He nods.) Oh, well, would you like to come to my apartment? For supper? I mean, I'm not suggesting a passionate evening.

GLEN:
Well, you made that clear. Yes, sure.

VALERIE (smiles a little):
Well, the chicken will be better warm anyway. It's an old French recipe. and—

COACH:
Is that really the end of your resistance, Glen?

GLEN:
I hate to say this, but I don't like chicken.

VALERIE (suddenly in the swim):
What do you like? Really, if you could have any

food at all, what would you choose? Maybe something you can't get in a restaurant.

GLEN:
Homemade vegetable soup. You know, the kind with rich broth and big chunks of beef stewed a long time.

VALERIE:
Oh, I'd love to do that. It doesn't seem like a company dish, or very sophisticated, so I haven't made it in years. Yes, I'd like that. We'll eat homemade soup and big pieces of French bread with garlic butter—

GLEN:
How about green apple pie?

VALERIE:
With whipped cream? I'll forget my diet and relax and gorge myself. I'm really sort of a sensualist. I love a huge meal by a warm fire in the living room, with some good music and plenty of wine and— maybe it will rain. I have some huge oak logs. I'm not strong enough to lift them, but maybe you—

GLEN (laughing):
Hey, I thought you were the one who didn't want a romantic evening. (The group smiles.)

VALERIE (a little miffed):
Well, who said I didn't like romance as well as anyone? I just don't like to be seen as nothing but a bedwarmer. (To the coach.) A bedwarmer would be a "thing," wouldn't it? I want some company. I want some exchange with a real person, someone I can communicate with. That's why I chose you.

GLEN (genuinely surprised):
You think I'm warm? Most people say I act sort of cold, because I'm quiet. Anyway, I was just kidding about having a romance.

VALERIE (now somewhat desensitized in her anxiety about the subject and able to talk about it; she speaks lightly):
I may look like an old woman to you, but I was telling the truth about what a lot of men want from me.

GLEN:
Hey, honestly, you don't seem old to me physically. I meant what I said about your figure. I really think you're damned attractive. At least, you attract me—especially now that you're saying real things about yourself and letting real feelings show in your face. Spending Sunday evening *alone* with you sounds good.

VALERIE (reddening a little with pleasure):
Honestly?

GLEN:
Honestly.

Much more than the making of a date has obviously taken place during this dialogue. Both Valerie and Glen have learned that they can express feelings of genuine attraction and resistance to virtual strangers. Their fears of rejecting and of being rejected have been reduced.

They also began to learn that elusive evasions and accommodations that masquerade as tact can be more hurtful by far than simple truth. They could see how evasions can lead to hidden fears and resentments later on. Also, they began to learn that they could express their fears and doubts and ask plainly if these feelings were based on reality. They learned that they should always *check out* "mind readings"—their guesses about what others think and feel——because these assumptions can be remarkably misleading.

An even more basic phenomenon that developed between Valerie and Glen was that they *leveled* with one another. And as they exchanged real fears and wishes, a chemistry arose between them. As the tension grew, they began to be attracted to each other as people. The role of tension and conflict is crucial to intimacy (see Chapters 11, 12, and 14). They began to care about one another, and so they reached beyond courting to become a pair.

This is not a chance occurrence. Virtually all couples who try the rejection ritual experience the same fascinating phenomenon of bonding, which is an early stage of intimacy. The Sunday date may lead to nothing more for Valerie and Glen, but they have learned how to induce intimacy in others.

It may be only a mild taste, a gentle stirring of warmth. But it is real, and the phenomenon appears so dependably in these exercises that a total rejection almost never occurs. Some degree of bonding, some sexual stirring, however vague, almost invariably emerges. We call it instant intimacy.

We would like to encourage readers to practice experiencing rejection in the interest of reality and to practice the flexing of pairing muscles. If you will seek out possible rejections from strangers, you can begin to deal with your fears of rejection from intimates. Besides, who knows? You may be misreading a potential intimate's apparent lack of interest. You need to ask in order to know for sure.

The reader can approach the person he trusts the most and say:

"I want to try an experiment with you. You know me very well and I trust you. I'll trust you even more if you tell me your reservations about me. I won't defend myself, but later maybe I'll tell you how it felt. To make it all fair and square, let's time your rejection of me and then I'll claim equal time to reject you.

"I want to do this with you for two reasons: I'll feel more at home with you when I know what displeases you about me or our relationship. Secondly, I want to toughen up. I'm too sensitive to rejection from everybody, especially strangers. I always blush when I am criticized and later I get angry. So I want to practice surviving rejection without fear or guilt. If you agree, I'll demand things of you and you'll either accept or reject my demands. Okay?"

"Beautiful people" especially need to practice this exercise to learn how to say "no" without guilt. Unless they can reject some of the many advances that are made toward them, they will become "things," used by everyone who finds them attractive. Learning how to reject and be rejected is important insurance against exploitation.

11

Aggression: The path to intimacy

WHEN Valerie and Glen struck a spark of intimacy, they became total personalities in each other's eyes, not merely co-members of a group. Human sympathy—in the literal meaning of the word, "feeling with"—was the inevitable result. They stopped seeing each other as things, and saw each other as people. They no longer viewed one another as segments (she-old, he-shy).

A segmental view of a person is not real. It is illusive. In part this illusion is a convenient excuse for by-passing some people since we cannot know and concern ourselves with the feelings of *everyone*. But this illusion is easily broken.

Suppose that Myra, the boss's secretary whom you see as a thing to facilitate your contacts with the boss, dissolves in tears as you pass her desk one morning. You stop and ask what's wrong. She says her mother has died, and weeps. You get her some coffee. You tell her how crushed you were when your father died last year. You share the bitterness of mourning. You put an arm around her shoulder. From that day on, there will always be a certain bond between you, an intimacy. You have revealed yourself to one another.

Something else is likely to happen. Myra now stops being a tool to manipulate in your relationship with the boss. You will now be able to level with her about many things, to tell her your genuine feelings and reasons when you need something from the boss. Ironically, you can now hope for more help from Myra when your needs are real, than you could in the past when you curried her favor with presents.

In a courting relationship, the illusion of segmentalizing usually breaks only by accident, or after long acquaintance. As an example, Ed has been going out with Cassie only every week or two. He thinks of her as the cute little thing who lives in the same apartment building. He likes to be seen with her. He likes to joke with her. And the same feelings motivate her to accept the dates. Both are lonely and like casual company for dinner now and then, or just to go to the laundromat with. They think of themselves as good friends, know many of the details of one another's lives, and have lately made love a couple of times. Yet their relationship is a segmental one.

Then one night Ed drinks too much at a party. He is not drunk, but his usual flip veneer cracks. He pours out his inner frustrations about his work, tells Cassie his real hopes, his real dreams, his hunger for a more meaningful role in life. Suddenly Ed is a whole person for Cassie. She feels warmth and trust, and begins to confide in him her disenchantment with the career-girl life, her longing for marriage and a family. An accident of alcohol has opened them to a chance for true intimacy.

In more casual contacts, segmental illusions can become as restrictive as handcuffs. People may develop very unfair conclusions about the characteristics of someone with whom they really would want to pair. When Cassie did not know Ed, and saw him first in the local laundromat, she rejected him out of hand because he had red hair and red-haired men had never attracted her; because he had not shaved and grooming is important to her; and because he was reading *Field and Stream* and she is not enthusiastic about outdoor types.

In reality, Ed was reading *Field and Stream* only because one of the articles interested one of his business clients, and he had not shaved because he had a dinner appointment that night with the same client; he wanted to be immaculate, and his redhead's skin would not tolerate two shaves in a day. When by accident Cassie got to know him, this much of the segmentalizing was broken: she learned that Ed was not an outdoorsman and not sloppy. And as she learned to like him, she began to think, "Red-headed men really look so lively and virile."

But accidents don't usually happen at just the right time to crack illusive prejudgments. Our clinical research indicates that the best way to break the segmental illusion and reach intimacy—as the gentle reader may be alarmed to learn—is *aggression*.

To many people aggression is inadmissible in loving relationships. When the senior author first presented his techniques of fight-therapy to the public, for example, he was told by some that true love was uncritical, that it needed no changes, that aggression connoted anger, invasion, pugnacity, and that these were the antithesis of love.

Yet all these unpleasantnesses are, realistically, part of love. For aggression arises whenever one's wishes and hungers are not recognized or respected. And when people love, or seek to be loved, inevitable frustrations arise as they reach for closeness, for sharing, for understanding and being understood. These frustrations, psychology has long known, must lead to aggression.

Before Karen started in one of our pairing classes, she had gone to a business convention. During one of the cocktail parties, she noticed an attractive man who surveyed her periodically, but looked away whenever she looked at him. After half an hour, Karen, who had over the years become impatient with courting-style games and etiquette, decided to forget her inhibitions and simply speak to the man.

KAREN (bracing herself):
You've been looking at me, and I've been looking at you, and so I thought I'd come over and talk to you. Do you mind?

VINCE (flustered and reddening):
No, no. I mean, it's great. It's fine.

KAREN:
I don't know what you must be thinking, but—well, I'm just awfully tired of all the nonsense between men and women. I think I might possibly like to get to know you, and you might like to know me. So I decided, well, suppose I just come and say so.

VINCE:
You know, I really had the same idea in mind. But to be honest, I just didn't have nerve enough. I do know what you mean. I get sick of the merry-go-round, and I think you must be quite a girl to take the initiative this way. You really have to have guts.

KAREN (blushing):
Thanks. (They look at one another. Both laugh self-consciously.) But now I really don't know what to say. I mean, I think of things, but they're not exactly real. You know what I mean?

VINCE (he stares for a time, and then nods his head):
I do know. (They grow silent again, and both look more and more uncomfortable.) I feel like sixteen years old. (There is another, still more awkward pause.) I have it. How do they work it in those psychological camps in northern California? You know, the ones where they get into a swimming pool nude with a bunch of strangers and then touch each other?

KAREN (reddening again):
Do they really do that? I'd think they'd feel ridiculous.

VINCE:
Well, I've read that's what they do (he winks at her and smiles broadly. (Say, how'd you like to come up and try it in my bathtub?

KAREN (her smile fades, and annoyance creeps into her voice):
Why, sure. Why shouldn't I accept a nice invitation like that?

VINCE (watching her uneasily, but trying to be light):
Well, why not? Of course, I don't mean to imply that you look as if you *need* a bath—

KAREN (angry and disappointed):
Why does every man have to fall back on the same old phony sex bit? Can't you be one man who sees me as something besides just a body to screw with?

I don't know quite why I'm so angry—I know that partly you're just joking. But I really get so sick of it.

VINCE (his own anger surfacing):
That's the typical female bit! You come over and make a show of being all frank and straight, and now look what happens. Why do women always have to push men into being some sort of department-store dummies? How can a man relax and be himself?

KAREN (angrier still):
Relax? If I relaxed with you, I'd probably find myself flat on my back in ten minutes, and I'd be lucky if I got a polite thank-you for it. Sure, I suggested that we could be honest. But then what do you do? You stay phony, the way men always do, so they can get what they want.

VINCE (getting quite angry):
Don't put all the men you know on *my* back! I'm me, Vince—I—(he stops himself. Hey, this is ridiculous. We don't have anything to fight about. We're acting as if we'd been dating for six months! (He smiles.)

KAREN (she returns the smile, embarrassed):
You're right. At least six months. I'm sorry I attacked you that way. I guess I was pretty nervous. You know, coming up to you and all that.

VINCE (soothing her):
Sure. I understand. It's just as much my fault. I got so edgy, I was tongue-tied for a while, I didn't know know what to say, so I tried to be cute. I'm sorry I got out of line. Listen. Let me get us a drink, and we can sit down and really talk. I don't know any of the

real things about you, your name, where you work, what you like, what you don't like. . . .

This couple had come remarkably close to reaching some genuine intimacy, not through knowledge or skill, but through sheer frustration. The frustration had produced aggression, a forceful driving toward each other.

Most people tend to think of aggression as the anathema of love and the destroyer of intimacy. For them, the word conjures up only images of fury and greed and uncaring self, of invasiveness.

We call this H-type aggression, or hostile aggression, and here is how it develops: If you hunger for something and reach toward it with great energy, and that reach is frustrated, you naturally become hostile. Your reach may be interfered with by something, or someone who does not want you to fulfill your need. Then your hostility is directed toward them. Or, you may yourself block the reach or not even allow it to begin. The frustration in this case leads to a slow-burning hostility, resentment. You may turn this against yourself, which leads to depression. Or you may become resentfully hostile toward a person who, you believe, is the cause of your denying your own reach for satisfaction.

What many people do not understand is that the reach itself is the purest form of aggression. When that reach is directed toward a human relationship, aimed at changing it or securing a reaction from a partner, then its goal usually is not to take or injure. Most often, the idea is to achieve *impact* on that partner. This is I-type aggression.

Impacting is a passionate assertion of self, a demand for recognition as a total person, not a thing. To feel the impact of one's personality, one's identity, on another is one of the greatest joys of pairing. It is the sense of having made valid and genuine contact. It is the recognition of having made impact that affirms one's existence, that validates one's maleness or femaleness and yields a sense of potency. It makes one feel real and alive.

When Karen suddenly and surprisingly confronted Vince, she was impacting. He felt the contact and responded with his own personality. But then, neither knew what to do. The ground and the feelings were unfamiliar to them.

Vince became so uncomfortable that he was forced to fall back on a more familiar style. He took up the classic male mode of sexual aggressiveness expressed with rough humor.

The moment Vince took this role, Karen felt thinged, as a sex object. Her impact, her personal assertion, seemed to be blocked. The frustration brought out her H-type aggression. She attacked. She retaliated by symbolizing Vince as "just another man." This, in turn, brought out his hostility.

Such an exchange, rather than being a disaster, offers a chance for real intimacy. But both Vince and Karen had to overcome a feeling of impropriety about their little scene. "I seemed so wrong," Karen recalls, "to have such an angry exchange with a stranger. Only now I realize that because we were being genuine with one another we were not really strangers. That was the beauty of it."

Although the sudden closeness made Vince wish he could retreat back to smooth courtship etiquette, Karen's genuineness made it impossible to regress to the usual chatter about favorite songs and favorite movies. Conflicted and frightened by their leap into instant intimacy, Vince nevertheless took Karen's phone number and, after a pause of a few days, called her to become friends.

This leap, past all the usual early coyness, posing, and secrecy into "instant intimacy," is an excellent antidote for the poison of thinging. The technique is quite easily learned and helps one to form and evaluate relationships with very great speed.

12

Polarity: The passionate difference

POLARITY, the attractive fascination of differences, is another key to intimacy.

Polarity is not so simple as the old saw, "Opposites attract." We do not recommend pairings of totally different personalities or life styles, which can make mutual understanding so limited that it is hard to progress very far in an intimate relationship, and harder still to sustain it for any period of time.

At the same time, an exchange with someone who shares virtually all of one's background and opinions will generate little chemistry. It is likely to be soothing and sweet, like a meeting with an old childhood sweetheart. But there is little excitement. And in the end, the result is likely to be boredom.

We teach students to look for disparities that create interest and excitement. Consider a meeting between a rancher and a poetess. At heart, they might share many appreciations, of the beauty of nature, the complexity and mystery of growing things, the fertility of the land. Yet each brings to the other a different and fascinating world. If their minds are at all alive and inquiring, they can make an extremely stimulating pair. The polarity between them might be the one of city versus country, or of abstract word versus concrete physical act, or even thought versus feeling.

Even if two people are in the same occupations and circumstances, for example, but in different towns, they can draw fresh perspectives from one another.

Some potential intimates hardly need to look for polarities. The differences are all too obvious between Northerner and Southerner, Jew and Catholic, old and young, black and white, native and foreign, rich and poor, conformist and eccentric, conservative and radical.

We do not encourage pairers to seek out such differences. But we tell them not to shy away from potential partners just because great polarities exist. When they do exist, we advise that the pairers not sweep them under the rug and emphasize whatever similarities they find between them. If the differences are confronted, the interest that is generated is likely to be warm and intriguing. The experience can be enriching because each is attempting to pair not only with an individual but with another world as well.

The strangeness of such a pairing can be frightening or at least uncomfortable. An Italian girl and a British man, for example, are likely to have very different ideas of the optimal distance they would like to maintain between each other. People must have a high tolerance for tension in such pairings. Their tolerance may increase in time, but we advise:

"If you find it too hot in the polarity kitchen, don't cook!"

The most obvious and powerful of polarities, of course, is that between male and female. One might suspect that this polarity would most easily lead to good pairing. But the matter is not nearly as simple as it looks.

To demonstrate this, we hold a session that we call The Gender Club. We go around the room, asking each person to list what they consider to be some good and bad qualities characteristic of the opposite sex. Try this exercise sometime, perhaps among a few friends. But do not be surprised if tension boils up quickly. For as each person makes his statement, he automatically *things* the members of the opposite sex, and they are likely to respond resentfully.

Science has found very few sex-linked characteristics that are innate, with the exception of the physical. At one time, psychologists agreed that aggression is a male characteristic. In recent years, investigators have demonstrated that even this is questionable, that aggression seems merely to be repressed in the woman by her culture. The senior author has clinically studied male and female fighting styles for years, and concluded that one cannot stereotype them. A woman may cry or scratch and a man may sulk, or hit, but the psychological differences between these fight styles are small.

The courting culture continues to encourage a belief in male-female stereotypes. As a result, many men and women use these false attributes to manipulate the opposite sex. To do so is to block all chance of intimacy. These tactics are easily unmasked, because sexual polarity is so important and impactful to most men and women that there is constant suspicion of its coy or dishonest use by either sex.

The vast majority of men are angered by such stale approaches as, "You're such a big, powerful man, and I'm such a weak little female, could you possibly help me to—"

Such dishonest gambits and, especially, premature sexual advances, instantly produce a feeling of manipulation in the person who hears them, together with enormous resistance against any request. Both males and females who manipulate by means of sexual polatiry generally *intend* to fail in developing any relationship. Most are nonintimate icebergs who actually use their "advances" to hold the opposite sex at a distance, while making an overt show of seduction and invitation.

The techniques used by men and women in these cases often address themsleves to fears that symbolize the most direct forms of physical sexual exploitation. For example, a characteristic male sex fear is castration, sometimes expressed as a fear of engulfment. The fawning male who leans all over female strangers at cocktail parties is stimulating his engulfment fear in order to distance himself from the women.

Women tend to fear invasion. A woman who is sexually afraid of the male is likely to respond to attempted intercourse with *vaginismus*, a tense closure of the outer vaginal musculature, that makes penetration difficult or impossible. Emotionally, this same sort of invasion may be threatened by a man at a resort bar, who, before any relationship can be established, suggests that a woman leave the door to her room open for him. He, too, is distancing.

Because of these fears, men who list their dislikes about women commonly describe many kinds of engulfing behavior, and women frequently list invasive behaviors among their dislikes of men. Each sex projects onto the opposite sex the kind of threat they feel within themselves, and this is an important kind of thinging.

In general, men and women who hold on to stereotyped views of their own sex roles and those of the opposite sex are poor bets for intimate success. We therefore encourage efforts to destroy such fixation. The best way to accomplish this, as with all illusions, is to test the reality of the situation.

Only when a man states a real fear, such as, "If I let you get close, I'm afraid you would start running my life," does a woman get a chance to reply, "But I don't *want* to run your life!"

We caution pairing students to think before they state reservations or stir up polarities that involve sex-linked characteristics ("Your blouse looks more like a man's shirt"). We remind them that each partner is an individual, whether male or female. There is a common tendency to lose sight of this simple, obvious fact and to resort to symbolizing. Sexual wishes and fears are so impactful that there is an extra-strong tendency to hide from them with illusions.

One of the most arresting and most troublesome sexual polarities is born of the usual difference between male and female strength. To reduce the woman's fears of male physical power and the man's guilt about the crude advantage that this strength provides, we introduce our pairing students to some simple physical games.

One of the best is "greaseball" which is played outside on a pleasant day. This exercise requires a softball and a clear, grassy area large enough for two "bases" and a "home plate."

Now partners can obtain more information about one another's sensitivity, readiness to respond, readiness to abandon self, sense of humor, courage, competitiveness, inventiveness, goodwill, pettiness, and ability to stick to rules. It is the kind of information that helps people to evaluate each others' reliability as intimates. One couple acts the role of opponents. The other takes the roles of coach and referee. The coach facilitates initial negotiations regarding handicaps, and may interrupt the exercise for renegotiations. The referee makes the final decision on any disputed points.

Handicaps are developed in order to equalize the physical differences between men and women players, so that the woman can exercise intensely with her partner without fear and with a realistic sense of possible victory. Also, once handicaps have been arranged, the man can use his strength fully without guilt. If either one wins too easily, it is because the handicapping is faulty; not that he or she is "better."

The partners strip to bathing suits, and the girl oils her body with lotion or cream as the first handicap. Other handicaps are negotiated and put into effect, such as giving the girl a head start at the ball.

At a signal from the coach both run at the ball and grapple for possession. The one who gets it takes off for first base. The other tries to get the ball away, but if the runner reaches base, he or she is "safe" for a maximum period of two minutes. During that time the runner decides how to get to second base, and the pursuer tries to anticipate any "steals." Gains are cumulative, so that if you lose the ball and then regain possession you can return to the base you held before your loss. The goal is to reach "home" base and the game is over when both partners have had at least one chance to carry the ball, and when the first one reaches home safely.

If you try this exercise, you will learn the value of working out conditions of equality as well as exploring any tendencies to cruelty in yourself or your partner. Some women try karate in the middle of a game; some men cannot resist the temptation to use a wrestling hold on their partners. All such behavior provides valuable data for future verbal confrontations (which should, however, not attempt to "psychoanalyze" a partner). Besides, greaseball is fun to play and hilarious to watch.

So is "Bacata," a hit-and-dodge game played with very softly upholstered bats—a modified version of a pillow fight. Although it is almost impossible to get hurt playing this game, we urge couples to discuss handicaps and agree beforehand on "surrender gestures."

Women quickly learn how to handicap their man so there will be equality in the encounter. He can be restricted in the space he may use. She may demand a "defense zone." The game is played until either party "gives up." Students are encouraged to observe their joy at being aggressive and to explore their feelings about "winning" or "losing" after the game.

Another strength equalizer is "Push Me." Again, handicaps are negotiated, this time in order to create a balance of power as the woman tries to push the man across a room and pin him against a wall.

The power of sexual polarity is so great that it usually manifests itself in time without any help. One of our students on an air trip chose a seat next to a young lady and then felt tongue-tied. He made a few statements of mild feeling—about being nervous on take-offs, about a ring she wore, about the clouds. But he could not seem to find a graceful way to express his real interest. (To do so is not always easy for beginners. They can block, hang up. But if they keep trying, such efforts usually become as natural as the feelings themselves; the practiced eye finds the way easily.)

After half an hour, the student was frustrated and annoyed with himself, which made him even less able to think. He was stirring his long legs restlessly in his discomfort and staring moodily out the window, when the lady solved the problem for him.

"Excuse me, but you look so uncomfortable," she said. "You're such a big man. I wonder if you wouldn't feel less cramped if you took my aisle seat?"

He began to laugh, for she had invoked polarity much better than he. He had ignored his obvious physical discomfort; she had turned it into effective polarization.

Relaxed now, he was able to express his genuine feelings about the incident. "I laughed," he told his seatmate, "because I've been sitting here for half an hour trying to figure a way to make you notice me and get you talking to me. I almost trampled three people so that I could sit by you, and—"

What girl would resist?

There is one important polarity that is frequently misconstrued as an issue to be emphasized and argued out. Many people feel that they should love as much as they are loved. This is another impossible dream, a matching that may take place in heaven, but not on earth. The fact is that at any given time in pairing, from the start, there is one who is more interested, more desirous, more involved, more committed than his or her respondent. We teach students not to try to equalize this difference.

Indeed, the gap can be *widened* by insisting that a partner reciprocate exactly. This pressure is alienating.

In a good pairing it is possible for one to care deeply and the other to be only decently receptive and responding, with enough support and response to keep love alive. The feeling of caring for someone is greatly valued in life and those who have it should not spoil it by unrealistic attempts at matching.

The phenomenon of polarization has good educational value for pairing students, many of whom start out with a faith in the sameness of matching. They learn that, similarities or differences, all is grist for the pairer's mill. The only requirement is that he be deeply committed and deeply involved in the creation of relationships for their own value.

13

First
impressions,
first
illusions

ONCE the techniques of instant intimacy have been applied, and an initial relationship is established, the sensitive pairer is wise to keep checking on whether illusion is creeping into the relationship. If illusions are not dealt with promptly, they can loom large with time. So the good pairer exchanges some first impressions with his partner.

There are many adages about first impressions, and virtually all of them prove to be correct.

We have conducted research to find out how people's impressions of one another develop and change, and how important first impressions really are. In one experiment, students in college dormitories were introduced to total strangers with whom they would be living. Then they were asked to write down first impressions. Some time later, the same students were given back these essays, with instructions to edit them in the light of what time and repeated exposure had taught. Again, at intervals, the students were asked to re-edit, to cross out errors, add new thoughts, or underline confirmed ideas.

The development of opinion stopped early. After three editings, there were few changes—except for random blow-ups. In many cases, changes were circular: first editings showed modifications, but later versions restored the first view. When Lew Hart, Dr. Bach's research consultant, used computers to analyze all versions, roughly two-thirds of the information in the final impression could be found in the first one.

Other work confirms these findings. People tend to freeze first impressions. Details, pro and con, are added. Some hidden weaknesses and attributes appear. But mainly, one thinks of others as one did on first meeting them. Initial illusions tend to be preserved.

Most people want to make up their minds, to get the picture, very quickly and end any uncertainty. Saddled with this tendency to freeze a fleeting impression into a firm judgment, pairers are asking for trouble if they try to live up to unrealistic expectations of a partner—by colluding or by illuding them. Sooner or later, the pair will become terribly uncomfortable. For to continue to win affection and approval, they will have to accommodate—to be unreal.

The importance of initiatory acts is illustrated by this complaint in a longstanding pair relationship:

DOUG:

I don't understand why you don't want to take the weekend backpack trip with Hal and Gwen. You know, it's been three months since we've been in the woods or the mountains? I really miss it.

HELEN:

Well, I was never that much of an outdoor woman, after all. I mean, I love the scenery, but camping out is pretty hard on a woman. It's different for a man.

DOUG:

But don't you remember what you said when we met on that Sierra Club Hike?

HELEN:

What did I say? That I loved the scenery? That I loved nature? Of course, I do. But carrying a pack is really exhausting for me.

DOUG:

But it seems so much like part of us—being alone in the wilderness. Remember how we slipped away, the two of us? Cooked our meals together? Made love in the open?

HELEN:

Well, what do you want me to say?

DOUG:

I don't know. You seem different now, somehow. It just isn't the same. That's why I want to get into the mountains with you again, bring it back, bring you back—

Plainly, Helen had allowed Doug to believe that she was far more of an outdoor woman than she actually was. Their initiatory experience had been the kind of thing she was not really prepared to sustain. She had been smitten with Doug, but she had not really been too happy with back-packing and trail living. Doug would spend every spare minute in the mountains if he could. Helen would be happy never to use a sleeping bag or cook over an open fire again. Consequently, Doug's initial expectation of them as a pair is now continually disappointed. But he has continued to cling to that image, and feels resentful toward Helen for denying it by her subsequent behavior; he sees it as being "out of character."

Similar problems might have developed in many other ways. Suppose, for example, that Doug had at first been a very relaxed, experiment-minded sort of lover, that his first sexual experiences with Helen had been played out over whole days or whole nights. But this had been for him a unique initial exploration, an exercise in sensuous curiosity, encouraged by Helen's unusually keen interest and her delight in sexual experimenting. It is not his usual style of making love.

Gradually Doug becomes restless about Helen's expectation that they continue to have long-drawn-out experiences. Now Helen is resentful. She thinks Doug is becoming perfunctory about sex. She begins to attack his sexual potency and his "waning" sexual interest.

Doug and Helen are saying the same thing to one another: "You cheated me. You led me to expect something other than you are. You have a different view of our pairing than I have."

Misleading initial acts, impressions, and images can become disastrous later on. But it is easy to replace them with reality by checking out and sharing first impressions as soon as possible.

So once intimacy has begun, the partners must clarify where they stand. This is simply done. First, the initial meeting should not end without a firm commitment for another, and a statement about what has happened.

Chad says to Doris as they part: "You know, I've never danced so much in one night. I'm not that good at it or that interested. But if I hadn't kept you dancing, you might have run away, and I certainly couldn't have held you for hours. It excites me, being close to you. But I'd like to talk and be close without having to count the beat. I'm really a clod on a dance floor, I guess."

She replies: "You're not such an oaf. I enjoyed the dancing with you. It's one of my things. And I'll bet you'd be good if I showed you a few little tricks. But I want to talk, too, and I admit I liked being close. I'm glad you took that dance—and kept it for two hours. And I'd like it if we could stop and dance just a little on Friday."

"Sure," Chad answers. "I'll give dancing, or anything else, a try with you—if you can stand it. I'll pick you up at six Friday night, and we'll drive to that seafood place at the beach. We'll have a chance to talk more. They have this warm deck with a sea view and afterward we can go someplace else."

This pair has arrived at a simple, unequivocal statement of where they are. Doris had followed her normal style of recreation, since she liked to dance a great deal. Chad had not. So he was wise to speak up about his typical style. Their initiatory act of extremely prolonged dancing is now recognized by both as unusual, not as a precedent. So there can be no resentment if it is departed from.

Chad has made it clear that he wants to concentrate on talking next time, and that he has expectations of physical affection. Doris has made it clear that this is fine with her, but that she would also like to dance a bit.

These are mild, but straightforward examples of assertive aggression. Chad and Doris have let each other know what each hopes for and expects of the other, and each gave the other a chance to object or to correct a false perception.

These rudimentary examples suggest how assertive aggression, the asserting of one's own perception of reality, prevents illuding or penetrates illusions that have begun. Assertive aggression is a continuing form of the impacting that causes intimacy to form and develop. Coupled with reality testing, which is really nothing more than the scrupulous checking out of one's assumptions, assertive aggression is the sure, but little-traveled road to a deeper intimacy.

14

Conflict: The key to sustained reality

AGGRESSIVE assertion of one's real feelings can do much more than forestall harmful illusion. It can, for example, keep small hurts and annoyances, born of carelessness and misunderstanding, from becoming buried resentments that build up to block a pair from real intimacy.

Unless you say "ouch," your partners cannot know that they are stepping on your toes.

Inevitably, pairing partners do things that offend one another and reveal irritating habits or points of view. Caring about each other, most healthy lovers would be glad at least to try to modify whatever bothers a partner the most. But most people are peace-loving. They tend to overestimate how much one can swallow and forget. Nobody likes to "spoil" a nice day or evening. But, like DDT, these irritations are not eliminated; they accumulate. By constructive aggression, pairers can ask for change, promptly, before anger mounts.

By asserting your identity, you preserve it and continue to have impact on partners, so that they know and respect that identity. If you continually compromise identity, it becomes eroded and confused. You feel smothered. Then the usual reaction is to push the partner away in order to gain breathing space.

One of the important uses of pairing aggression is to set a comfortably compromised distance between the individual lives of the partners. Each needs breathing room, enough elbow room to move freely, time alone to refuel—otherwise a partner can change from a desired lover to a resented jailkeeper.

Aggression assertion is also the only effective way to win real inclusion in another person's life and to become central in his thoughts and feelings. (This does not mean exclusive. Only the neurotic demands to be an entire world for the one he supposedly loves.)

There are many other uses for aggression. Sometimes it is nothing more than what we call *leveling*, an impactful frankness. At other times it means demonstrating the open transparency that can be so powerfully attractive in the beginning of a pairing and generate an attractive force for a lifetime as well.

It is this frankness, this assertiveness, this expressed hunger for being recognized and respected and real, that the senior author has popularized for educational purposes as "intimate fighting." His widely used fight-training system is a way of controlling assertiveness so that it is fair and not hurtful and does not deteriorate into destructive nagging and squabbling.

Passionate assertion is useful only when both partners express their demands and needs. These expressions are bound to conflict. That conflict can be healthy as long as it takes place under control, and need not injure. The fight system slows down the collision between identities, puts it into slow motion, so that what could be hard blows become, instead, forceful appeals to reason and good will. Constructive fighting draws good pairers together. It reassures and builds trust, for it keeps the partners real and understandable to each other. Its intent is neither to wound nor to "win," by outdoing the other. In fact, the system equalizes the partners, so that one is not strong and the other weak. For intimate love can survive only when both partners respect one another as peers.

The fight system is detailed in the senior author's earlier popular work, *The Intimate Enemy*. We cannot outline the entire system here. But in making intimacy grow, in resolving problems and conflicts, and in evaluating pairing relationships, we will frequently refer to the use of aggression. So we will highlight the basic principles of pairing conflict to allow the reader to put them to work.

Peter and Cathy came to the Institute to try and rescue a highly rewarding pairing that threatened to break down. They had recently had a terrible fight in the old no-holds-barred style of infuriated lovers. They were still angry and suspicious. They told Dr. Bach about the fight, and he then had them conduct the same fight in a systematic, noninjurious, growth-producing way.

Here is a reconstruction of the original battle, a painful Donnybrook. Cathy and Peter had been paired for some months in a close and supposedly exclusive way. But for more than a month both had been feeling uncomfortable, dissatisfied. They were upset about this decline from a very passionate beginning. Their lovemaking had begun to fail at times. Both sometimes were reluctant about seeing one another, but kept this secret. They were starting to feel tense at times when they were together.

Cathy was twenty-six and had never been married. Peter was thirty-four and divorced. Sexually ardent, Cathy had gone through a number of affairs. Peter had become rather promiscuous during the later phases of his breaking marriage and mistrusted himself because of this. He tended to be rather jealous, and with seeming tact, questioned Cathy closely about what she did during his occasional business absences that usually lasted several days. He had just returned from one of these engineering-sales expeditions when the explosion came. They had finished dinner at her apartment:

PETER (proudly):
I've been saving my good news for dessert. I closed the Comstock deal. Tyler called me in today and congratulated me himself. He said that one more like that and they'd just have to let me take over a department. Openings are coming up.

CATHY (genuinely pleased for him):
That's wonderful, dear. Do you get a big raise? You really deserve one.

PETER:
I'll get something; I don't know how much. But it isn't the money—though I know you're used to fancier dates than I can afford, with my alimony and child support.

CATHY:

I don't care about that, darling. I keep telling you. But I do wish you didn't have to be away on weekends. I get pretty restless sitting home on my days off.

PETER (knowingly):

Well, you didn't sit home last night, at least. I started trying to call you at four in the afternoon, and I tried up to one in the morning. (He studies her.)

CATHY:

Oh, for God's sake, not again! What do you expect me to do? Yes, I went out. Is that against the law?

PETER:

Probably shopped in the afternoon . . . (He tenses.)

CATHY:

Well, yes. (Impatiently.) And I got my hair done.

PETER:

And then you went to dinner, I guess.

CATHY (tightening; getting up to clear the dishes):

Yes.

PETER (trying to seem casually inquiring):

With your sister?

CATHY:

No. Do you want more coffee?

PETER:

No, thanks. With Joan?

CATHY:

How about an after-dinner drink? I've got some Grand Marnier.

PETER:
Okay. I see you're splurging. That's over your usual budget, isn't it? And you've already had some. Drinking alone?

CATHY:
Damn it, Peter, cut it out!

PETER (sounding injured):
Cut what out?

CATHY:
You know goddamn well what you're starting. No, I did not buy the cordial. Okay. It was a gift. Okay? So just stop playing detective. It drives me crazy.

PETER (he goes into the kitchen and turns her around, holding her arms):
What are you so defensive about? Where were you last night, while I was working in Cleveland?

CATHY:
Are you going to let go of me?

PETER:
Dammit, stop evading me!

CATHY:
All right, Mr. Prosecutor, the booze came from an old friend who took me to dinner and a play last night. Okay? I knew you'd get upset about it. Did you have to drag it out?

PETER (backing up just one step, his face darkening):
What old friend? Must have been a pretty good friend.

CATHY:
It's none of your business. (Coldly stares at him.)

PETER:
It *is* my business. Who was it?

CATHY:
I'm not married to you. Get off my back. I was bored to death yesterday. I got a chance to have some fun for a change, and I took it. That's all. It was harmless.

PETER:
You don't have fun with me?

CATHY:
Not when you're in Cleveland, I don't. Satisfied?

PETER (coldly):
Who was it?

CATHY:
No one you know.

PETER (tight with anger):
Cathy, I have a right.

CATHY:
Oh, no you don't. I'm the one who has the right. I have a right to have friends besides you. I'm young. I have a right to go out on Saturday night. I'll bet anything *you* were out boozing it up on your expense account.

PETER:
Dammit, you know the customers expect to be entertained.

CATHY:
And what do their wives do?

PETER:
Joe and Ted brought their wives along. I took them

to dinner, and to a bar with a combo. Hell, a lot of the time we talked shop and the three girls talked—

CATHY (furious):
THREE girls? Why, you—Roasting me like that when you're out with somebody else! I could *kill* you! That really tears it! You pompous, holier-than-thou—

PETER (shouting):
For God's sake, shut up and listen! Joe's wife just brought her sister along, and I— Who were you with?

CATHY:
Cliff Richards! He was down from Chicago, and he called me. I don't care now. You can know, you hypocrite.

PETER:
One of those guys in Chicago you used to screw with, isn't he?

CATHY (shouting):
You bastard! At least I wasn't two-timing my wife the way you were. I loved Cliff, and—

PETER:
And every other man in Chicago. Do they *all* call you whenever they get into town and want to get laid?

CATHY:
Get out of here! Get out!

PETER:
Maybe that's why I turn you off in bed, lately. You're so tired from good old Cliff, and good old Tom, Dick, and—

CATHY:
I hate, you, you bastard! I trusted you. I told you everything—Get the hell out of here!

PETER:
You slut! And feeding me his booze, to make me feel like dirt. (He grabs the bottle and starts to pour it down the kitchen sink. She snaps it away from him, and throws it at him, missing, but splashing him.) Why you little bitch—(He raises his hand, then wheels and slams out of the apartment.)

This fight involves many of the most common problems of pairing, including the respective rights of the pairers, the abuse of trust, as well as the partners' distance, individuality, independence, and how central each is to the life of the other. This makes it informative but it also makes for bewildering confusion between the pairers. One can see that each is trying to express important feelings, that these are expressed in muddled terms, and that neither really is hearing the other.

Yet such "blow-ups" may signal not the end, but only a need for change and improvement in communications. The fighters say to one another: "That was too much, too painful. Let's cool off and sort things out. What do you want from me?"

The elements of a fight such as the one between Cathy and Peter can be sorted out and controlled. With coaching, this conflict became a fair, noninjurious experience for both and led the pairing to growth and progress, instead of destroying it. Peter and Cathy are now in Dr. Bach's office nervously stealing glances at one another.

DR. BACH:
Now, let's see. Which of you two would like to

begin? Under our system, one of you would tell the other that he or she has a gripe.

CATHY:
He started it before, with his dirty mind.

PETER:
MY dirty mind! At least I don't—

DR. BACH:
Hold it. This is not a boxing contest; it is an attempt to have communication and reality. All right. You, Peter, begin by stating your gripe, and—

PETER (interrupting):
That will take at least an hour. But basically, this is all about Cathy's immature, irresponsible—

DR. BACH: (raising his hand for a halt):
No, no. Never like this. We do not label. We do not sit in judgment. We state a *specific* source of dissatisfaction. First we meditate for a minute, quietly, to find in ourselves what the specific thing is that really bothers us. Try that. Then tell her.

PETER (complies):
All right. Cathy, it really bugs me when you see other men. I love you, and you say you love me, but you won't be just mine.

DR. BACH:
Ah! A demand for exclusivity. Now, Cathy, when we hear the gripe, we feed it back, as exactly as we can. This slows things down. It also makes us listen, instead of just waiting for the other to stop so that it becomes *our* turn. Please do so.

CATHY:
That seems pretty silly. But okay. Peter, you are saying that it bugs you if I have any friends, and—

DR. BACH:

No, no. You must feed back exactly. What you have done in your minor change is to shift the meaning quite a bit.

CATHY:

It bugs you when I see other men. You love me, and I tell you I love you, but I won't be just yours.

DR. BACH:

Very good. Now, if this is what bothers you, Peter, some change should make you feel better. Tell her the change you would like.

PETER:

But that's obvious, isn't it?

DR. BACH:

Nothing is obvious in pairing. Tell her.

PETER:

Cathy, I want you to stop dating other men. Wait now. There must be something else.

CATHY:

You want me to stop dating other men.

PETER:

It's funny, I had this whole complicated thing in my mind when I came in, you know, about your attitudes and such, but this is all I can think of just now.

DR. BACH:

It's really not so funny. This is what tends to happen when we meditate on finding specific demands for change. Now, Cathy, you have heard and fed back Peter's demand for a change. Do you want to make the change?

CATHY:

No. I do not want to stop dating other men.

DR. BACH:

Feed it back, Peter. Then it will have impact on you.

PETER:

You do not want to stop dating other men.

DR. BACH:

We appear to have an impasse here. But maybe there is a way to compromise. Peter, is your demand negotiable? Are you willing to compromise in some way?

PETER:

How can I compromise?

DR. BACH:

Well, you could find out how much other dating she wants, and perhaps agree on some kind of limitations that would satisfy you both.

CATHY:

I don't want any limitations. I want to be free. I think this is really what it's all about. Peter wants to own me. It makes him angry when his property isn't safe.

PETER (protesting):

That's not true.

DR. BACH:

You hear, Cathy? He says you're wrong. You are making assumptions. Also, you are mind-reading him, really mind-*raping* him. This will only make him angry. We must state only what we know. If we have an assumption, a hypothesis about the other person, we must check it out by asking. It's all right to read minds, but only if we ask permission and get it. Otherwise, when we tell someone what they think or feel, we are engaging in the practice of what we call crazy-making. It is maddening.

CATHY:
All right, may I read your mind, Peter?

PETER:
I suppose so.

CATHY:
I think that you want to own me. You want to do whatever you feel like, without any commitment to me, but you want me safely on the string.

PETER:
That isn't true. I can be loyal to you. That business in Cleveland really was what I said it was. I admit I'm tempted a little by other girls. I'm human. But I'd rather give them up to keep you exclusive with me.

DR. BACH:
What about the commitment she says you don't want to make.

PETER:
Well, that's it. I'll be exclusive if she will.

DR. BACH:
We have a negotiating offer, Cathy. What do you think?

CATHY:
That's not a commitment, as far as I'm concerned.

PETER:
Well what would a commitment be?

CATHY:
There's only one kind of permanent commitment between a man and woman, even though I know that isn't always so very permanent.

PETER:
You mean marriage?

CATHY (dropping her eyes):
I guess so.

PETER:
You mean you want to marry me? Now I've told you that I have to—

DR. BACH:
Check it out, Peter. Is that what she means?

PETER:
Is it?

CATHY:
Yes.

PETER:
But you said you didn't want to marry me.

CATHY:
Because you said you didn't want to.

PETER:
No, I said I couldn't. I explained about the alimony and the child support. There's just not enough left for us to live on decently, until I get that promotion and the raise.

CATHY:
Then if you can't be committed, why should I be?

PETER:
I still say, there can be commitments other than marriage, just two people promising each other—

CATHY:
I've had that kind of promise in the past, in Chicago, and I wound up out in the cold. I commit myself, and then, when the man finds something he likes a little better, I get dropped. I guess I just want it all, or no commitment. I get too dependent. I don't really want anyone else, Peter. I didn't go to bed with Cliff. I didn't want to. But it made me feel good to go out with him. Free. Free of you.

PETER (hurt):
I didn't realize that you thought of me as just a ball and chain. I'm sorry.

DR. BACH:
You're mind-reading, Peter, without permission.

PETER:
Well, is that the way you see me?

CATHY:
No. And yes. I guess I mean it frightens me to be so very dependent on you. I'm afraid I'll lose you.

PETER (brightening):
Really? But I'm afraid of losing you. That's why it scares me so when you go out with other men. I'm afraid I don't have enough to offer you, to hold you.

CATHY:
Then why don't you want to marry me?

PETER:
I've told you and told you. The money. I *want* to.

CATHY (alert and delighted):
You mean that?

PETER:
Yes.

CATHY:

Then why don't you tell me?

PETER:

Because of all *your* talk about independence all these months. I thought I might frighten you off. Do you really want to marry me?

CATHY:

Oh, yes. (She pauses.) I mean, on the one hand, I really want it very much. But then you—well, you do get so possessive, or something.

DR. BACH:

Cathy, it sounds as if you might have a gripe, and perhaps a demand for change of some kind. Do you think you should tell Peter about it? (She nods). Well, meditate first, and then perhaps this counter-demand will really clear some things up for us.

CATHY:

I'm not really completely clear about this, Dr. Bach. I know what I feel, but it's hard to express. I'm not as good with words as Peter is. If we argue about anything, he always seems to get his way. He talks me into it. I get exhausted and give in.

DR. BACH:

This is a fairly common situation, Cathy, when one person is more verbal or expressive than another. So what we try to do is balance the situation. We try to give the less verbal partner a chance to express what he or she feels without words, and without a distracting response from a partner who may be more clever with words. Would you like to try this, Cathy? There is no talking involved at all.

CATHY (looking doubtful, but somewhat relieved):
I would, very much. I get terribly frustrated when I
try to make my ideas stand up against Peter's.

DR. BACH:
Very good. One of our methods of nonverbal expression is what we call *molding*. One partner molds the
other into an expression of what he or she wants the
other to be in relation to themselves. Then the mold-
er—we sometimes refer to him as the Pygmalion—
places himself in a position which further clarifies
the relationship that he wants in the pairing. But if
you want to do it, Cathy, you must ask Peter's
permission first. We never assume the right to
manipulate or mold or invade another.

CATHY:
May I do this to you, Peter?

PETER:
Yes, dear. I want to know what you feel, and sometimes it's frustrating when I feel you can't tell me.

DR. BACH:
All right, Peter, then stand up and close your eyes.
Please remain completely silent until this exercise is
completed. Then you can open your eyes, and you
will both have a chance to discuss the result.

Cathy, you may place Peter in any position you
like. You can adjust his clothing, if he doesn't object,
make him lie down, stand, kneel, whatever pleases
you. You can also arrange his facial expression if you
choose.

Cathy leads Peter by the hand to the center of the
room. She looks up at him. He is seven or eight
inches taller than she. Following Dr. Bach's instructions, she closes her own eyes and meditates for a

moment, to let her feelings come through clearly. Then she smiles, as if she has the idea she wants.

She takes Peter's hands and puts them in his pockets. Then she studies him. She advances and lifts the corners of his mouth into a small, gentle smile. Stepping back, she looks up at him again, in a mildly dissatisfied way. Then she approaches and makes him kneel.

Now Cathy kneels in front of him. She straightens up as tall as she can. Kneeling, they are now close to being equal in height, she a foot or so away. Then she shakes her head and slowly backs up, until she is about three feet away from him. Now she smiles affectionately and extends both arms to Peter, but does not touch him.

CATHY:

You can open your eyes now, Peter.

PETER:

(He does, and looks a little puzzled.) I'm not sure I understand.

CATHY:

Well, think about it.

PETER:

You've brought us down lower and made us more the same height, more eye to eye. Does that mean you want us to be more nearly equal?

CATHY:

Yes, that's right. But there's more. There's a more important part.

PETER (studies the situation):

Why did you put my hands in my pockets? (He thinks about this.) Is it so that I can't touch you?

CATHY (a little uncomfortably):
Yes.

PETER:
But you're reaching out to me. Yet you're just far enough away so that you can't touch me. I don't think I get it. Do you mean you really don't like our physical relationship? (He asks it anxiously.)

CATHY:
Oh, no. You know I don't mean that. I love being physical. It's my best way to tell you how I feel. And you're a good lover. You're so affectionate.

PETER:
Then—what? I know I touch you a lot, more than you like sometimes?

DR. BACH:
Has she said so?

PETER:
Sorry. Do I? Touch too much?

CATHY:
Not that. I like to be touched. It's different, what I mean.

DR. BACH:
If you're not sure what her molding means, Peter, perhaps you'd better ask.

PETER:
Yes. What does the rest mean, Cathy?

CATHY:
You get so close. It's funny, but I can say it now. Sometimes you make me feel surrounded. That's why I put your hands in your pockets. So you

couldn't hold me, and I could reach out for you, when I was ready. That's why I backed up, too.

DR. BACH:
Why don't we all sit down, now, and Cathy, perhaps you have a demand for a change, too, that you can express.

CATHY:
It's still hard to pin it down. But it's as if Peter came too close, for too long.

DR. BACH:
Tell Peter, and try to be very specific.

CATHY:
I guess my gripe is that you seem to want to spend more time together than I.

PETER:
You think I want more time together than you want.

CATHY:
Yes. I'm afraid that if I say I'm bothered, that you'll think I don't love you. But I need time to myself.

PETER (he first feeds this back):
When do I do this?

CATHY:
Weekends, for example, we're never out of each other's sight. We sleep together Friday night, and then stay together all weekend. I need time to breathe. In a way, I'm relieved when you go out of town.

PETER: (he shows that he has listened first, by feedback):
I thought you liked the closeness. I know I've asked you.

CATHY:

You've asked if I liked the things we did together, if I liked sleeping with you and eating meals with you and going to museums and things. I really do. I like it all. But not all at once, not all of the time.

DR. BACH:

Well, what sort of demand do you make, since Peter seems to accept your complaint as valid?

CATHY:

It's hard to be specific. But I would like it sometimes if you would leave me a few hours on a Saturday and Sunday just to do my thing quietly, wash my hair or drip-dry my blouses, little chores I haven't time for during the week. My poor apartment has been a wreck for months. Or I might just like to read or watch television. You're a little too much for me. I'm exhausted by Monday morning, when it's time to go back to work.

PETER:

I know I do this. And the truth is, it tires me out, too. I see you getting restless, and when I do, it makes me feel anxious, as if you don't like being with me. So I cling all the harder. Maybe it would be good for both of us. I haven't been to a ball game for four months, for example.

CATHY:

Then you wouldn't mind giving me weekend afternoons or mornings to myself? I mean, you won't be hurt? I think maybe that's another reason why I keep wanting to escape to someone else. It makes me feel pressured to be so close.

PETER:

Let's try it out, and see if it doesn't help. Do you think it will, Dr. Bach?

DR. BACH:

I think so. One of the common differences between people is the problem of distancing: how much room each wants to allow the other or take for himself. You, Peter, seem to want much more closeness than Cathy can take. People in love often fear they will be engulfed, that they'll be overwhelmed by the partner, and exploited, if they give too much of themselves. Cathy has already expressed fears of exploitation, which seem to stem in part from past bad experiences, and in part from now knowing where she stands now. I think, by the way, that this may be what she means when she says she wants a commitment from you. Is that so, Cathy?

CATHY (she nods):

I can feel a great difference already, now that Peter has really told me more about how he feels.

DR. BACH:

You know, both of you, that you never really finished the fight for change that Peter began? I let it go unresolved, because I did not think it could be settled until Cathy could express more of her feeling. But what are you going to do about that? You had both taken non-negotiable positions about whether or not she could date other men.

PETER:

I got the impression that you changed your mind, Cathy.

DR. BACH:

Mind-reading, Peter! And you don't need to read her mind. You only have to check out your assumption.

PETER:
Have you changed your mind?

CATHY:
Not really. Dr. Bach is right. I do feel more commitment from you when you level with me. But I still want to be free to keep my friends and see them. Maybe I will and maybe not.

PETER:
But Cathy—

CATHY:
You see, if I promise, it can only be that I won't go out with anyone, not that I won't want to.

PETER:
You mean I just have to trust you?

CATHY:
No more than I have to trust you in Cleveland.

DR. BACH:
Can you compromise your original demand, Peter, now that you have more information and understanding?

PETER:
Well, I do understand Cathy's point of view better.

CATHY:
But I want to know if you really accept it. Or will you just resent everything? Givng me more time to myself, leaving it open about whether I see male friends—

PETER:
We can try it out and see. (He thinks a moment.) One thing that would certainly help is if I can believe that you will keep me posted on what you

do—especially if you want to be with someone else because they mean more to you.

DR. BACH:
Excuse me, Peter, but is it possible that you could phrase this question differently—that you are only asking Cathy to be open and level with you?

PETER (thinks it over):
I guess that really is what I mean. Will you, Cathy?

CATHY:
Of course, now that I start to feel that I can level, without your being angry or rejecting me. When you're open with me, it makes me trust you.

This fight is quite a discursive one. The reason is that so many problems existed in this pairing, unresolved, merely swept under the emotional rug. But the fight provides a number of suggestions about how self-assertion and leveling can handle many difficulties.

Among the basic principles demonstrated by this fight are these:

1. Be specific when you introduce a gripe.
2. Don't just complain, no matter how specifically; ask for a reasonable change that will relieve the gripe.
3. Ask for and give feedback of the major points, to make sure you are heard, to assure your partner that you understand what he wants.
4. Confine yourself to one issue at a time. Otherwise, without professional guidance, you may skip back and forth, evading the hard ones.
5. Do not be glib or intolerant. Be open to your own feelings, and equally open to your partner's.

6. Always consider compromise. Remember, your partner's view of reality may be just as real as yours, even though you may differ. There are not many totally objective realities.

7. Do not allow counter-demands to enter the picture until the original demands are clearly understood, and there has been clear-cut response to them.

8. Never assume that you know what your partner is thinking until you have checked out the assumption in plain language; nor assume or predict how he will react, what he will accept or reject. Crystal-gazing is not for pairing.

9. Don't mind-rape. Ask. Do not correct a partner's statement of his own feelings. Do not tell a partner what he should know or do or feel.

10. Never put labels on a partner. Call him neither a coward, nor a neurotic, nor a child. If you really believed that he was incompetent or suffered from some hopeless basic flaw, you probably would not be with him. Do not make sweeping, labelling judgments about his feelings, especially about whether or not they are real or important.

11. Sarcasm is dirty fighting.

12. Forget the past and stay with the here-and-now. What either of you did last year or last month or that morning is not as important as what you are doing and feeling now. And the changes you ask cannot possibly be retroactive. Hurts, grievances, and irritations should be brought up at the very earliest moment, or the partner has the right to suspect that they may have been saved carefully as weapons.

13. Do not overload your partner with grievances.

To do so makes him feel hopeless and suggests that you have either been hoarding complaints or have not thought through what really troubles you.

14. Meditate. Take time to consult your real thoughts and feelings before speaking. Your surface reactions may make something deeper and more important. Don't be afraid to close your eyes and think.

15. Remember that there is never a single winner in an honest intimate fight. Both either win more intimacy, or lose it.

While some new partners suppress tension and conflict in order to cement the new relationship, others deliberately create fights. Typically, new lovers who are not yet sure of each other, argue a lot about what appear to be trivia. Deliberately or intuitively, they do this to gather "intelligence" about each other. They may even pose completely hypothetical conflicts to find out what the new partner would do if, for example, a rival suitor were to appear.

They may also criticize each others' tastes in clothes, choice of movies, etc. Once these imaginary or exaggerated conflicts have been handled in a bonding rather than tearing way, intrinsic tensions arise from the "I-and-You" relationships.

Typically they deal with such basic dimensions of intimacy as: "I'm not important enough in your life; I don't like being a side issue." Or who "wears the pants." Or setting the conditions under which others are to be included ("Strange that even at Christmas you didn't take me to meet your folks"). In realistic pairing both the initial apparently trivial and extrinsic conflicts as well as the later and more obviously significant intrinsic conflicts deepen intimacy because of the style of conflict management we teach.

We can even generalize that freedom from conflict is practically always limited to partners who act out well-defined roles under explicit contractual conditions. Examples are: tennis pals and smooth but highly specialized "Good Time Charlie" relationships between playboys and playgirls.

Sometimes one partner creates and or reinforces self-deprecations. These are not tensions and confrontations focused on legitimate "I-and-You" conflicts, but alienating, ego-downers. Some examples are: "My God, the way you stumble when you walk!" or remarks about "The way you frown," or "The way you never read any books."

There are many other refinements to the system of intimate aggression. But this basic outline is enough to start any pair toward the constructive uses of aggression, toward the piercing of illusions and the reaching of reality.

15

Is it love—
or
exploitation

ONE of the more common questions that psychotherapists hear from single patients is, "Doctor,, do I really *love him* [or her]?"

Much energy goes into the search for this answer in the early phases of pairing. Unfortunately there are no neat scientific answers. There are many levels of love, as Rollo May has pointed out, and the same word is often used for all of them.

"Do you *feel* in love?" the psychotherapist may ask. "Then you are. But the really important questions are: Is this love really rewarding, or does it punish and deprive? Is it capable of deepening to true intimacy, or will it merely result in your exploitation?"

Possibly an even more common question asked of the psychotherapist is, "Does *he* love *me?*"

The answer, again, is usually much the same. But will he love you in order to use you? Is he genuine or a pairing con man? Is he capable of becoming intimate and really desirous of being so? These questions, too, can be answered.

In general, such questions can be answered by testing the reality of what you see, hear, feel, and think about the relationship and the partner. You can probe what may be illusions with constructive aggression. If you assert your real feelings in an informed way, and check all assumptions religiously, you will find out what is real, what is illusive, or the result of the mutual anxious collusion.

Andrea did not realize for a long time that she was being exploited. She and Fred met at an antique swap meet—both loved things with a feeling of history—and quickly learned that they had many tastes in common. Since both believed that such matching is a realible guide to pairing potential, they began dating steadily.

Andrea and Fred fantasized together a great deal —for example, about the colonial house they would find in the country, run-down but original, and would restore. They spent many afternoons hunting through junk shops for overlooked antiques and then refinished and repaired them. They had real camaraderie, a real sense of sharing, and they began to talk about opening a shop together.

"It promised to be a real partnership," Andrea told Dr. Bach, when she came to the Institute. "Oh, there were flaws. We drifted into sleeping together, but neither of us got terribly excited about it, though it wasn't actually bad. It was comfortable and comforting, very sweet and warm.

"We told ourselves we were glad there was no frantic quality about our sex—the I can't-keep-my-hands-off-you sort of thing. We decided that we were so made for each other, so alike that our feelings had to be calm and relaxed, as if we'd been married for twenty years.

"Fred loved to have me take care of him, and I loved to spoil him—you know, cook for him and straighten up. And I liked the way he valued what I thought and asked my opinion about everything; what suit to buy, what to take for a cold and things like that. He'd been married a long time and simply couldn't do for himself.

"Then a few months ago, I came down with infectious hepatitis. just before Christmas. Fred come to see me at the hospital just once. He called me every day and said how busy he was. He was trying to clear things up so he could go back to Iowa for the holidays to visit his parents.

"I'd planned to make the trip with him, but it was starting to be clear that I could never make it. Finally Fred called me, very nervous and depressed sounding. He said it was foolish, wasn't it, to deprive his parents of his Christmas visit. He didn't really want to go, he said. He had been in the dumps ever since I'd got sick. But what kind of Christmas could he and I have if he stayed? Would I mind terribly much if he was selfish just this once?

"I told him to go ahead. It was typical of him to discuss something, anything, with me before making a decision. And it always seemed to make me say yes. After all, I wasn't a child anymore. His arguments were very logical, and we could have many Christmases together."

"Then he called again and said he had a lovely present for me, and he'd bring it to the hospital the day before Christmas. The afternoon of that day he called again. His plane reservations had been scrambled, and he would just have time to get to the airport. Would I forgive him if he sent my present by messenger? Then suddenly I realized that he hadn't got to the hospital once in the past twelve days, and it was only a short cab ride away. In the middle of saying, 'Just have a lovely Christmas for me, and wish my best to your parents,' everything cracked. I yelled at him, 'Go to hell!' And I smashed the receiver down.

"As soon as he came back, and I was well, Fred started calling me every day, two or three times. I won't see him because I feel he made a fool of me somehow. But honestly, I don't really understand what happened, what our relationship was. I just know it wasn't—healthy."

For several months, Andrea dated anyone and everyone who asked her, but she could not forget Fred, who phoned, wrote letters, sent flowers, pleaded, and threatened. When she eventually joined a pairing class she was urged to bring Fred with her. But after half an hour, it appeared that they could not get a real fight or real exchange going. Neither could seem to verbalize what they demanded of the other.

Again, nonverbal expression was tried. We had the pair use an exercise we call *Slave Market*, for we suspected what the problem was. One of the pair becomes master in this exercise and the other is slave for a short period of time, usually two or three minutes. Then the roles are reversed. The master may order the slave to do anything reasonable, fetch and carry and perform other little services. The exercise shows partners that they can surrender by agreement, rather than as an accommodation or out of weakness. It trains them to be explicit about what they want from the other. And sometimes it leads to the discovery of a partner's hidden assets.

By mutual agreement, Fred became master first.

Many people are shy about being master, but Fred took to it with ease. His manner was immediately one of command.

FRED:
Andrea, remove my shoes. Now rub my feet. Harder. I've been standing all morning. Now take that cloth and polish my shoes. Quick now. Get those specks by the heel. Good. Now come behind me and rub my shoulders. Ah. Yes, that feels very good. And—

When time was called, Fred looked genuinely disappointed. Now it was Andrea's turn. She seated herself and meditated, to try and think of what she wanted Fred to do. Finally, she shrugged, and then asked for time to begin.

ANDREA:
Fred, would you please bring me my purse from the table? Please, Fred don't walk so slowly. That's not fair. It uses up all the time. (Fred grins puckishly, and then walks still more slowly.) Come on, Fred. Please. (He brings her the purse.) Thank you. Now I'm the master, so you have to sit at my feet. (There is a long pause.) I can't think of anything, Dr. Bach.

DR. BACH:
Just relax and listen to your inner feelings as the master.

ANDREA:
(Complying.) Please warm my feet, Fred. They're cold. (He does so.) That's it. Just hold them while you sit on the floor in front of my chair. Ah, that's good. Now let's see. (Pauses.) I can't think of anything. Oh, yes. Put your head in my lap. Fred. It

211

feels soothing. (She sits out the rest of the time in this way.)

DR. BACH:
Now, how did you like these experiences, Andrea?

ANDREA:
I guess I really don't like being the master too well, though in some small way it's nice to have Fred being a little attentive to me. And I didn't mind the slave part at all. Probably (she smiles at Fred) because it's you. It's fun, really.

DR. BACH:
And you, Fred?

FRED:
Oh, I enjoyed the master part of it. It felt very natural having Andrea take care of me. She used to do so much of it. It's never bothered me to have Andrea do for me. But I didn't care for the slave bit very much. I kept trying, frankly, to avoid it, to make a joke out of it. Every time Andrea ordered me around that way, I felt a sort of inner resistance, a kind of resentment, I'd almost say.

After this ritual, Fred and Andrea could be guided to communicate somewhat better. They were asked to engage in a practice fight for change, using real feelings and their real circumstances of course. Fred's gripe was Andrea's withdrawal from him. His demand for change was that she begin seeing him regularly and often again.

Andrea acceded, with the reservation that Fred must come to pairing classes with her, to try and help her straighten out her sense of uneasiness about their pairing. Fred agreed. Andrea had trouble making a complaint and demand for change specific enough. Then, after some deep meditation—

ANDREA:
You know, Fred, I've suddenly had an insight. I think it was partly seeing you fresh after so long, and partly it was the master-slave ritual. But I seem to have pinned down a feeling—the awful angry-frightened feeling I had that day in the hospital. I had some of it again when you asked me to start seeing you again. Maybe this is really more of a reservation. Anyway, I had the feeling that I was being used, exploited. I was angry with you for doing it, and frightened that it might always stay that way with us, and ...

DR. BACH:
Let's keep it to the here-and-now, Andrea.

ANDREA:
Sorry. But I have that feeling again today, and that's my gripe.

FRED:
I wasn't exploiting you, honey—Don't be so sensitive.

DR. BACH:
You deny any responsibility for her "gripe." Right? But you admit her feeling is genuine, yes?

FRED:
I hear you say you feel that way—okay. What change do you want?

ANDREA:
I want you to agree that you won't insist on my coming to your apartment, so I won't fall into the

trap of being your housekeeper again. That way maybe I won't feel you're taking advantage of me.

FRED (after feeding back):
Good God, Andrea, you always said you liked looking after me. (He sounds outraged.) I don't see why we should put ridiculous restrictions on—

DR. BACH:
Unfair fighting, Fred. You have no right to label Andrea's reservations as ridiculous. And never mind what she always used to say. Respond to what she says *now*. Check out anything that puzzles you.

FRED:
Don't you think you'd enjoy looking after me now?

ANDREA:
In a way I would. But I think I'd feel exploited. If you come to my apartment, by the way, I'm not going to cook for you all the time; I want to go out to dinner more.

FRED:
Well, that's all right. But it's practical for you to visit me sometimes. I have so much more room for working on furniture and such. I have the tools, and the antique books. Don't you think it's practical?

ANDREA:
Yes, I do, really. (She thinks.) All right, I'll offer a compromise. I'll come to your apartment if you agree that when I do, I'm a guest and you're the host.

FRED (suddenly impatient):
I'm sorry Andrea, but I think this is ridiculous. It's too rigid and there are too many arbitrary rules. (He becomes quite irritable.) It's ridiculous.

ANDREA:
I know you don't like rules. But please try this. I want to be with you, but I can't continue in our old way—I get scared.

FRED:
Well, I guess I'll have to try it. But I have to say that it all feels terribly unnatural somehow—artificial.

ANDREA (smiling):
It makes me feel very good for some reason. Thank you, Fred.

Andrea's intuition had been shrewd. Fred was a mother's-little-boy. He showed this by welcoming every chance to order women about, to sit back and relax while they slaved for him. He also revealed it, in later discussions, by a tendency to ask *permission to be naughty*, as when he asked to be excused from standing by Andrea when she was ill, abandoning his adult responsibilities toward her to go off on a holiday. Mother's-little-boy, moreover, always becomes anxious and depressed when a mother surrogate such as Andrea is ill, and he is threatened with the loss of her caretaking. This is why he was so eager to go home literally to Mother in Iowa for Christmas. And why going to the hospital to see Andrea was unbearable for him.

When he was separated from Andrea, he had frightened her with some of his calls, talking much about his pitiful state, his poor meals, and dirty laundry. Twice he even discussed suicide. Such a reaction is the result of a common and severe pairing problem, an inability to reverse roles, in this case to become the caretaker at times. It sparked Andrea's intuitive withdrawal and placed important limits on their pairing potential.

Curiously, Andrea had limitations that in some ways paralleled Fred's. She had a lesser degree of Daddy's-little-girl syndrome. Originally, she wanted to be with Fred almost constantly. She became heavily dependent upon him and freely invited the exploitation she got. She had some difficulties in role-reversal, too, but they were masked by her motherly reactions, which were really ways of binding Fred to her by making him dependent on her.

With therapy, Fred and Andrea were eventually trained to reverse roles to some extent. But the need for such training, the warp in their relationship, would not have become apparent to them if Andrea had not at last asserted her fears that she was being exploited. And she had carefully suppressed these feelings for a year and a half, with the illusion that she and Fred were close pals, who enjoyed "playing house."

Exploitation is largely the result of thinging by one or both partners. A lover becomes a tool, a facilitator who makes it easier for the exploiter to satisfy some need.

Healthy pairings also include facilitation. But in exploitative pairings, one or both partners are seen *primarily* as tools, not people.

Fred saw Andrea as mother, free housekeeper, nurse, supporter of his antique ventures. When she became seriously ill, she had to abandon all these roles. At that point not very much was left of her that mattered to him. Fred became anxious and depressed, because his facilitators had been taken away. He was less upset about Andrea's illness than about his own loss. He did not want to see her. To do so would have freshened his anxiety and sense of loss because he did not know how to relate to her outside her usual roles as an object.

The exploited partner in pairing usually has an intuitive feeling that something is wrong, a vague sense of being used, a feeling of not being recognized as a person. But he prefers to avoid checking out his feelings; he is afraid he will find out he is not really loved as a person, and does not want to face the possibility of separation. So he sets up or accepts illusions to cover his fear.

Andrea adopted a common illusion that goes something like, "See how Fred needs me? So he must love me. At least, he can't do without me."

She then unconsciously kept expanding her role as facilitator, to bind Fred more and more to herself. To Andrea, Fred was also something of a thing. At thirty-two, she was tired of the anxieties of the dating game and wanted someone to hold onto. This need made her slow to face reality.

Andrea's assertion of herself forced Fred to see her as a person. As soon as she faced her fear of exploitation, she could test its reality by refusing to do those things that made her feel exploited, particularly keeping house at Fred's apartment. Fred immediately became anxious and angry when she told him she would no longer do these things, but would see him. For he did not get back most of his lost facilitation. He got back mainly the whole person, which was not his primary interest.

The case is reported in detail to demonstrate that it is not difficult for assertive aggression to break through to reality when exploitation is suspected. And it almost invariably *is* suspected by an exploiter's target.

Any pair can conduct the "Slave Market" exercise for themselves without supervision, although it is usually best practiced in the presence of another couple who also want to undergo this reality test for themselves. In either case, a full set of ground rules must be negotiated in advance and mutually accepted. Both partners must get a turn. A turn should be no longer than two or three minutes. If one partner is skeptical about the procedure, he will warm up better (and the exercise will be mutually more rewarding) if he takes the first turn. Some typical rules are: "No genital sex" or, if the exercise is done at the beach, "Nothing that gets me wet."

When pairers become masters, most of them seem to ask for back-rubs or make demands such as "Dance and sing for me, entertain me," "March up and down and salute," or "Pick me some flowers." No slave need perform even a legitimate master's command. Any order may be ignored under the rules, but only if the slave is willing to add another two or three minutes to his slave-time.

Probably all pairings carry with them some fears of exploitation. And probably all partners can benefit from testing for it and eliminating the destructive seeds sown by thinging. When the doubts of exploitation are removed, trust blossoms, and the way to deeper intimacy opens wide.

16

The sexual expression

THERE is no more dramatic and explicit playing out of the male-female relationship than the sexual act. Each act is a little microcosm of the relationship. So when men and women master the art of emotional authenticity with one another, they are also able to master the art of authentic *sexual* expression.

Sex as an expression of meaningful pairing is particularly rewarding. But it would be naïve indeed to believe that it is the only rewarding sex. For since we know that truly intimate relationships are rare, we would then have to believe that the vast majority of all intercourse was unsatisfying, hardly an acceptable idea.

The fact is that sexual activity has a virtually infinite range of meanings and rewards. With our pairing students, since we assume that their training guards them against neurotic and illusive forms of sexual expression, we find it is necessary to make clear distinction between only two basic kinds of sexuality—sex as an expression of real intimacy and sex for its own sake.

This differentiation is hardly a new one. It has been pointed out for years as a matter of adult choice by such responsible psychologists as Rollo May, Erich Fromm, and the late Abraham Maslow.

Although it is plain that intimacy-based sex has a far deeper and more significant meaning in the lives of pairers, scientific investigators have had to reject the old idea that sex *without* intimacy cannot be satisfying or have validity of its own. The reason for differentiating is not to point to one as good and the other as bad. It is to help our students avoid unrealistic expectations.

In spite of traditional moral disapproval, sex for its own sake, nonintimate sex, is rapidly becoming more common, especially as an exploration by young adults. Temporarily, it can deeply absorb and involve the partners. And from a psychological point of view, it is not damaging provided that it is authentic in its own terms; that is, if neither partner is manipulating or tricking the other into the experience by misrepresenting his feelings. Once again, reality, recognized by oneself and expressed to the other, is the best protection against guilt, anxiety, and anger.

On the other hand, our clinical experience shows that sex for its own sake does not bear much repetition. Both men and women report that they usually have little interest in repeating nonintimate sex experiences with the same partner.

The mature adult finds that nonintimate sex begins to pall rather quickly, to become routine and mechanical, to provide little real uplift after the excitement of the moment. While initial sexual acceptance can be very meaningful indeed for the exploring young, its impact declines with each incident.

One of the realities of sex without intimacy is to accept the limited impact that is likely to result. Another is that *instant sex is not instant intimacy*. In fact, the effect is usually quite the contrary. The likelihood is that instant sex will retard or prevent intimate development.

Since initiatory acts and impressions tend to make deeper and more lasting impact than do later ones, instant sex generally means mutual segmentalization, mutual thinging. Both partners tend to become sexual facilities. Psychologically, it is very difficult to reverse initial imprintings of behavior, attitude, and expectation. They tend to become frozen. It makes little sense to freeze solidly a kind of relationship that one does not want later on. If the hope is for intimacy, it is wisest to cultivate that intimacy first, not to make sexual things of oneself and one's partner.

Yet sex can be curiously unpredictable. We have seen instant intercourse mature into true intimacy more than once. We suspect, however, that in such cases there may have been enormous initial impact that preserved the partners as people.

When our pairing classes enter into discussions of sexual confusions and hang-ups, we sometimes help them to relate their questions to other aspects of pairing. We ask: "*When* should one make love? When does making love enrich and bind—and when does it take away, and alienate?"

Of course each pair creates a unique sexual relationship. But these questions elicit a welter of confused ideas about conventions, taboos, and mixed emotions that can be clarified. After the students have, in round-robin fashion confided stories of their own satisfying and unsatisfying sex experiences, a pattern begins to take shape that becomes clear to everyone and provides guidelines for future choices.

Beverly is speaking up in such a discussion. "I had a strange experience a week ago," she said. "It embarrasses me to tell it, but I'd like to understand it.

"I'd been dating Ed for months. I liked him, but there hadn't been any big passion thing. He didn't make any demands on me, though he'd been asking me lately to go away with him for a weekend. Then he asked me to go to a weekend house party in the desert. It sounded like a really great weekend with about six couples, and I knew some of them.

"When we got there, Ed and I were shown a room to share with a double bed. I started to back off. But—well, I don't know. We'd already had some cocktails and were relaxed. I didn't want to make a scene with this very liberal crowd. I didn't want to embarrass Ed, and so on. He immediately said he didn't know it was going to be this way, and I believed him. He said he wouldn't put pressure on me.

"But when bedtime came—well, it was pretty hard to avoid. I'd been feeling depressed about my recent divorce, and lonely and wanting affection. And Ed was very affectionate and gentle. There was no seduction nonsense; I just went ahead.

"That was Friday night. Saturday morning, I woke, and there he was. We looked at each other, and I really felt dislike for him, and I could tell he wasn't overjoyed with me. The sex had been perfectly good. But neither of us felt we ought to be there, I guess, and maybe resented the other a little for the fact that we didn't feel comfortable. What surprised me was all the affection I'd felt for him seemed to be gone—just like that.

"I started to follow the principles I've been learning, to say what I felt. But the timing was wrong. Ed didn't want to talk. I think he really didn't want to say that he was feeling much as I did. We were supposed to stay that night, but instead, we made an excuse and left in the afternoon."

At that point Dr. Bach broke in:

"That's not all there was to this. In using the words 'wrong timing' you indicated that you were allowing yourself to be caught up in a manipulative program. You did not follow the principle of confronting and exposing what bothered you about his insistence on having sex."

"I thought I did say what I felt," Beverly said.

Dr. Bach asked: "Did you also see that you colluded when you went along with Ed? And didn't you string him along for months?"

"Well, I needed affection and companionship," Beverly said.

Dr. Bach said: "Yes, fine, but it didn't work for you. Your bed accommodation backlashed. By permitting sex to be imposed on what for you was a social friendship, you terminated a socially pleasant companionship that may have had future intimacy potential."

Beverly went on: "Yes, I guess I ruined the whole thing when Ed didn't want to talk. Well, the next day was Sunday and I went off to the beach to be by myself and try to figure out why this old friend should have become so unattractive to me. I was sitting on the sand, looking out to sea, when Tom came up. I didn't know his name then. He sat down nearby, and after a while, we started talking.

"In a little while, he was really pouring things out

to me. His wife had died a few months before, and he talked about all the things he missed and all the things he felt. And I started talking about my divorce, and how I also felt a kind of mourning. We both dumped it all out for what must have been three or four hours. Then we went swimming, and touched quite a lot, and when we came out, he asked me to go back to his motel room, just like that. He was in California on a business trip from Boston.

"There were no apologies for asking, no should-we-shouldn't-we talk. And I never even hesitated. We made love for hours and hours, and I don't know when it's been so great. Then I left, and he's back in Boston. I don't even know if I'll ever see him again.

"My point is this. I squirm every time I think about that night with an old friend like Ed. I feel—wrong about it. I really regret it. But I'll always remember Tom and feel very content and right when I do, even though I was picked up by a stranger on the beach. Am I some kind of nut?"

The class quickly picked up the essential differences between the two experiences. The relationship with Ed, while long-standing, was nonintimate. But through the mutual exchange of deep feeling, the strong wish for genuine human contact, Beverly and Tom had established intimacy almost instantly.

The sexual experience of that intimacy felt as natural and simple and appropriate as the verbal expression. And it was entirely natural that it worked just as well.

Many people have an unfortunate tendency to regard sex as a separate entity of life. But it is an expression, one way of reaching to another human being, of sharing feelings. When sex is expressed in a pairing, in an intimate relationship, it is authentic behavior, with all the rewarding characteristics of other intimacy.

Intimate sex is part of the pairing system—exciting, but not anxious. The partners trust one another. Feelings and motivations are open. And so there can be no sense of exploitaton, of being used as a body, a thing, a sexual implement.

The perennial question of our pairing students, "To bed or not to bed?" is safely answered this way. When sex is authentic, in terms of the pairing principles, it is likely to be rewarding and not to leave any unpleasant psychological hangover the next morning. The courting system places an excessive risk on a couple. It asks them to venture into a fantasyland, where the realities of skin and taste and scent are likely to clash with the illusions that the partners have built up about each other.

When a couple seeks to express an unreal, illusive relationship, they seem to require a perfect setting to act out their fantasy. No matter how good a setting they find, it will probably provide some minor distraction that breaks the spell and spoils satisfaction. It is enough for a dog to bark, a child to cry, a mattress to squeak. These simple distracting realities remind: "You know what we're doing is not entirely genuine. You're not a dream lover; that's just a role you're playing."

Another increasingly common form of fantasy sex is that of the growing autonomy—or independence—cult. This kind of relationship achieves physically satisfying sex by, in effect, denying the existence of a relationship with the partner. It excludes the partner from one's personal sexual equation with the idea, "You do your thing, and I'll do mine."

Psychologically, this is a form of masturbation, the

sex mode of the isolated. In a sense, one had merely learned to use a complex machine to satisfy one's autosexuality. But once such sex is over, its effect is not unlike that of drinking. The cocktails caused pleasant intoxication for the moment, perhaps met some special need, but there is no intoxication now.

The accommodation, illusion, and deception of courting-style love are particularly evident in the sexual arena. For both men and women are especially anxious about sexual matters. The threats are, of course, explicit. Both partners must expose themselves, visually as well as in terms of adequacy and potency, and these are matters of concern to everyone. Then the woman must allow herself to be invaded, and the man must allow himself to be engulfed. Fears of exploitation and rejection are heightened. The temptation to illude oneself or one's partner becomes enormous.

The free exchange of feelings between pairing partners furnishes the trust that is essential to reduce anxiety in this vulnerable situation. It is far easier for the pairer to feel that he is approaching sex appropriately when his partner can say straight out what appeals to her, what her sexual wish is. ("Be gentle with me tonight." Or, "I really feel earthy after that movie. Be quick and hard.")

Genuine freedom of communication is the best possible psychological assurance of good sex. Pairing partners can tell each other what is good and how it makes them feel. They can let each other know if they become uncomfortable. So the partners begin to feel free and grow willing to take some risks, because they know that they will be told if some flight of sexual imagination does not please. And they have a way to work out the inevitable conflicts of taste, wish, and attitude.

It is interesting in this context to note the standard pronouncement of most sexologists—that sex is a major source of conflict in intimate relationships. This statement—which probably stems in large part from puritan roots—is upside-down. *Conflicts*—mismanaged or ignored—are the source of conflicts. Sex merely provides an especially fertile field for the revelation of conflicts that have been hidden or denied and left unresolved. Partners may manage the illusion that all is lovingly well in other ways. But in sex the truth tends to emerge in a merciless manner. The common effort to pretend that all is smooth as long as the love-making is good is soon doomed. Even if the sex remains successful, in the long run the human sense of reality is not fooled or lulled by physical affection. And more likely, the sex will be bled to death by buried resentment.

So the pairer learns not to try and hide from reality in a mist of phallic pleasure. And he learns to confront and deal with those conflicts that are peculiar to sexuality.

For example, take the common and often troublesome conflict of "will we or won't we?" Frequently, one partner is much more interested in sex at a given moment than is the other. And because sexual refusal can be so troublesome, one or both partners are tempted to accommodate and fake desire.

Tony arrives at Janet's apartment for dinner in a state of glum exhaustion, having been caught in a serious error at the office. Janet has had the day off, is relaxed and amorous. She embraces Tony warmly the moment he enters.

In a courting relationship, Tony, afraid to seem rejecting, may accommodate, feigning interest that he does not feel. He is hungry, he needs a drink and half an hour's rest. But he goes along, only to make himself feel resentful. He may well strike out at Janet later over "nothing," or perhaps express his resentment during the act itself by "inexplicably" losing his potency.

But in pairing, Tony wisely states his feelings, knowing that Janet will be both accepting of them and open about her own feelings. Perhaps he says: "I know I'm really beat when *you* can't turn me on. I've had a rotten day, and I'm going to need a little time to get over it so that I can appreciate you properly."

Janet may be disappointed. But she is not hurt or resentful. Because both have been consistently open, she does not doubt her sexual competence with Tony, or her ability to have sexual impact on him. So she can say with a mock-rueful smile: "I'll wait—but just a little while. Why don't you have a nice relaxing bath, with a drink, and I'll come in and wash your back while you tell me about it."

Another delicate area of sexual conflict is that of aggressive dominance. When one feels sexually aroused, it is common to want that sense of arousal to have impact on one's partner. Sometimes mutual impact aggression is workable. But many people need to be more aware of their own sexual aggressiveness than of their partner's, in order to mobilize their strongest sexuality. Here conflict may begin, if both want to take an aggressive role simultaneously. We call this a sexual traffic jam.

Courting-style partners are likely to compete until one of them submits, often resentfully. But pairers can reveal and work through their aggressive feelings, and we have found that they can negotiate role-reversal. ("You take the lead tonight, but tomorrow is my turn.")

Aggressive dominance can be calibrated through

such intimate negotiations. Pairing partners learn and accept the idea that the stereotyped associations of masculinity with aggression and femininity with submission are not eternal truths. They learn that either man or woman can, in the immediate moment, wish to assert sexual aggression or be its recipient—and that this wish is likely to shift from time to time, even repeatedly within a single sex act.

But courters are often so conflict-phobic that they are ultra-cautious about expressing sex aggression, or about asserting any wishes that vary from their personal pattern. Their anxiety leads them to form such paterns quickly, making sex rather dull, and often in terms of cultural stereotypes.

"Hey!" he protests in alarm. "What are you doing? The man is supposed to be on top."

"Yes, I wanted to make love last night," says she. "I gave you several little clues. What else can a woman do, come out and say she wants it, or just start doing it?"

Pairers are not so role-bound, or so bound by habit patterns. We do not teach general sex techniques because what works for one pair may not for another. But we do help each pair to discover which techniques are most fulfilling for *them*, by integrating candid aggression with spontaneous affection. The result is a good sex life kept interesting by unrestrained imagination.

Because feelings are stated openly and acutely—in contrast to the old belief that discussing sex destroys its romance—partners can say what they want, say what turns them on or off, and even say "No," without fear or guilt.

The psychotherapist knows from his patients with what craftiness an outspoken request for oral or anal intercourse can be used by a manipulative partner for a put-down, or a way to achieve control. But pairers openly agree that nothing they ask will be given to them as a resentful accommodation. They disavow the courting commonplace of "Submit now and collect later."

One of the first responses when a couple begins to learn the pairing system is sexual growth. Richard, for example, believed the fantasy that really good sex ends in mutual orgasm. He and Eve, who climaxed erratically, making such mutuality very difficult, were fighting about this when they first came to a pairing class.

One of our principal teachings about sex is that orgasm should not become the focus of attention, that it should not be sought as the Holy Grail of sex, and particularly not as the relative rarity of simultaneous orgasm. We have found that orgasm is best reached when the partners do not strain for it. We encourage, instead, an overall awareness of the immediate sexual present with its increasing tensions and sensations. Demands for cooperative action should be clearly cued, with aggression impact.

Preoccupation with orgasm thwarts it and leads to many sexual abuses and manipulation. For example, today's greater sex knowledge has led to the intimacy-destructive testings of the orgasm-watchers, who, as Rollo May points out, no longer ask "Will she or won't she?" but "Can she or can't she?" And one might as well add, "And with how many contractions?"

When Richard and Eve finally began frank discussions of their sexual responses to one another, *both* finally admitted that they had been trying to live up to the demands of *his* false sexual ideal by faking orgasms.

With coaching, both agreed they should stop faking anything and begin to share with one another what each genuinely enjoyed. They not only agreed that they enjoyed *sequential* orgasms more, because they were enabled to perceive fully both the pleasure of giving and that of receiving, but that they greatly expanded the variety of their sex. Much of that richer variety became possible through their learning to cue one another clearly and immediately when the actions of either distracted from the rising orgasmic tension.

Perhaps the richest reward of sex based on pairing intimacy is that the act tends to be more satisfying because each partner knows surely that he has had real impact on the other. The verbalizing of authentic feelings before, during, and after lovemaking tells the pairing lover that his sexuality is pleasing and effective. It validates the pairer as a man or woman in a most basically reassuring way.

But above all, the shared feelings, the shared sexual expression, celebrate the pairing.

17

Detecting
and preventing
exploitation

THERE are specific relationships that aggressive pairing is designed to detect and prevent. Some of them are sketched here. The reader may recognize familiar signs of his own relationships or feelings, or of his partner's behavior because elements of these relationships, while often unconscious, are common. Only the rare reader will fail to find some in his own experience. Their discovery should encourage reality testing, but not produce alarms that the couple faces certain disaster.

THE TAXIDERMIST AND THE STUFFED PAIRING

This is probably the most overt of thinging relationships. One partner "stuffs" the other, dresses him, arranges the expression on his face and then displays him. The air of the mortician's parlor that hangs over this kind of relationship is no accident. For in a psychological sense, the taxidermist must first "kill" his trophy. He suppresses its personality, so that it cannot appear to the world, or even to him, except in ways that create the impression he wishes it to make. The taxidermist uses his partner much as a hunter uses his trophy, to say to himself and perhaps to others: "Look at what I've been able to do!"

Ernie, who spent his childhood years in a foster home, has been seeing Harriet, a painfully shy girl, for almost a year. He places very few demands on her, but those he does make are stringent. He treats her in a rather formal, courtly way, which makes it easy for her to acquiesce to his style.

Ernie explains that he is chained to his job and works much of every weekend, so he usually sees Harriet on only one weekend night. Then he takes her out to dinner and some entertainment, spending quite generously. "I've never been to so many nice places in my life," Harriet boasts to her friends.

They almost never go to parties, except for a few large company affairs and to Ernie's college alumni functions. They rarely get together with another couple. When they do go to see people they know fairly well, Ernie thoughtfully gives Harriet several warnings long in advance. He attentively helps her decide what to wear, reminds her to get her hair done and has even helped her shop for clothes.

Harriet, whose formal education was limited, is flattered that Ernie's conversations with her are sometimes highly intellectual (they are often followed by reading recommendations) and that he discusses details of his work problems with her. He told her that he loved her almost from the first, but he does not offer much affection, except when they go to bed, which they now do once a week. Harriet is almost content with this, for she wishes no great closeness.

Their sex is quite perfunctory, and she never climaxes. Ernie says he is disappointed about this and tells her that it must be the result of her childhood problems. He gives her books to help her improve her attitude and technique. Sometimes he tries to arouse her by showing her erotic literature and pictures before they make love.

In the last few weeks Ernie has begun to talk about marriage; he says he should think about having children. He has discussed this with Harriet in a very sensible fashion, saying he would expect her to quit her job as soon as she was pregnant, that they would buy a suburban home, and he would commute. He has assured her that he would make few demands except that she devote herself to being a wife and mother. Harriet has begun to feel a sense of panic that she cannot explain. She wants marriage and a family very much. And no one has ever treated her as respectfully and considerately as Ernie. What, she asks, can possibly be wrong with her?

Part of what is wrong is that Ernie is the most flagrant sort of segmentalizer. To him, Harriet is a symbol through which he assures the world, and himself, that he is quite able to have a male-female relationship. Actually, he is an intimacy cripple, whose ability to love was never allowed to develop by his foster parents.

However, Harriet was not merely a victim; she had been born into a family where intimacy was not practiced. She is therefore intimacy-phobic, at least to some extent. It is a sound psychiatric principle that a victimizer cannot operate without the victim's permission. Harriet accepts Ernie's thinging because she, in turn, things him. Her reward is that he does not come too close to her. On the other hand, she senses that Ernie really has little interest in her as a person and is troubled because their relationship does not blossom. She is able to grow and wants to. She likes Ernie's proposal of marriage and children but she doesn't want a stuffed family run entirely according to his all too businesslike rules.

Harriet should have insisted, early in this relationship, on occupying considerably more than a one-night-a-week segment of Ernie's life. She should never have allowed him to chain her away from the normal social relationships that good pairers build. And she should not have permitted him to thing her as a symbol of his sexual competence, colluding with him to the extent of letting him become her sex coach.

The pairer who feels he is being stuffed and mounted should confront this feeling and check it out with his partner. Since most taxidermist-type nonintimates have a rigid, ritualistic way of pairing, the partner usually develops a strong sense of wanting to "do something different for a change." This is what finally happened to Harriet, and she came to us for assistance.

With guidance, Harriet was able to test Ernie's position. "I'd like our relationship to grow," she told Ernie, "and I'm afraid that you may not want this. I'd like to test it by doing some different things with you. Will you spend a whole day with me, instead of just an evening? And I'd like not to make up or have my hair done. Maybe we could go out into the woods together and maybe make love there. I think it might make me feel more free. Will you agree to let me plan some weekends?"

Ernie became nervous when he heard this. That night he drank quite a lot, made very brusque love to her, and finally agreed. He would let her know when he had the time. Then there was no further word. He appeared to have forgotten.

Helped by Dr. Bach to look into her true expectations of her relationship with Ernie, and to express these feelings in class, Harriet invited a couple to dinner and then called Ernie to tell him. Though they had a date that night, he called and excused himself at the last minute, saying he had to work late.

Harriet finally had to face the fact that Ernie was not going to accept any expression of her own self. He would not live with any change in the roles he had laid down for them, and he flatly refused to go to pairing classes to discuss anything.

Harriet had acted too little and too late. Instead of airing her resentments aggressively, she had "gunny-sacked" (stockpiled) them. At her last meeting with Ernie, her gunny-sack of complaints burst at last. When she had reached the level of a genuine rage, he looked at her coldly, shook his head and left. She never heard from him again.

Note that Harriet did not test Ernie surreptitiously. She openly announced her gripe, her demand for change and the need for a test. Manipulation cannot be broken by countermanipulation. If Harriet had not opened up, she would have remained Ernie's stuffed trophy even longer.

The taxidermist is easily exposed. Once confronted with real feelings and wishes, freely spoken, he does not reciprocate. He is more likely to examine his partner's feelings. Real feelings discourage him because they are dissonant to his attempts at trophy-stuffing and dummy-making. How can he arrange a dummy if it moves in ways *it* wants, saying what he does not want it to say, and actually changing from time to time? In short, if one does not behave like a thing, one cannot possibly be treated as one, any more than a lively puppy can be kept in a paper bag. It breaks out.

THE PRIVATE FREEDOM CULT

It is hard to argue with a woman like Terry, when she says: "No relationship is good if the partners aren't free. If they can't be individuals, they go stale and have nothing to give each other. That's what's wrong with most couples today."

Mark agreed. It followed that there was to be no exclusivity in their relationship in bed or out. She wanted no commitment. She wanted to stay loose. Dates should be broken even on short notice if either partner felt he did not really want them. In a museum, Terry might say, "You keep looking at Flemish painting; I'm going to the Egyptian Room." And she was irritable if Mark said he'd go along.

She told Mark she loved him. Sometimes she acted this out sexually, with wild abandon; twice she made love with him all night. But at other times she was repelled by his smaller physical affection, and became angry when he touched her. Her capacity for excitement turned Mark on. But he felt rejected when she asserted her independence.

She began mentioning other dates that she had on these independent days. Then one night in bed, she mentioned something amusing that a male friend of hers had said at breakfast that morning. When Mark protested, she reminded him of her previously announced credo, and of the fact that he, too, was free.

"The only way I can live with or love someone,"

she said, "is with no questions asked, no questions answered."

On the other hand, she assured Mark that he was really central in her life, that he was her real love. Lately, she had been saying this more and more often. Also, Terry called on his time with less and less warning. She would phone on an impulse to suggest seeing a movie in an hour, or to make love right away. Mark was afraid to reject these overtures. Even if he had plans, he would break them. For Terry responded to any hint of refusal with something like, "Of course, you *should* do what you most want to do right now." But her voice was cold.

The situation was maddening for Mark. He was involved in a totally undisciplined pairing. The partners made no attempts to calibrate their real wishes. It seemed to Mark that he was being used, that Terry wanted him at her beck, while claiming freedom for herself and giving only lip service to *his* freedom. He allowed this to continue against his own better judgment but ultimately came to us for advice.

A few weeks later Mark was able to tell Terry that he wanted to test his newly stiffened backbone. Terry seemed merely amused. When Mark flatly refused some of her last-minute summonings, she verbally shrugged the refusal off. As usual, she treated Mark coldly on these occasions and he would relent for fear of losing her.

Finally, he made a testing demand. If he was really central in her life, if she really loved him, Mark said, he felt entitled to reserve some prime time for himself. He wanted her to spend weekends with him. She argued. Mark merely said he would accept whatever decision she made and that this would indicate to him the reality of their relationship. She became very irritable but assented. They made a date for Friday night a week in advance, quite unusual for Terry, who said she hated commitments and thought that life was much richer when lived by impulse and surprise.

Friday at seven, Mark was at her door. She did not answer the bell. He used his key and found a note. "Had to go out. Sorry. Terry."

Mark waited three hours before he left, never to see her again. He had the answer.

Terry is an "autonomy worshipper." This is another, sometimes intractable, form of being nonintimate. The autonomist seems to be the reverse of the taxidermist. But in the end, the opposite-seeming behaviors yield much the same result: a relationship of tyrant-to-subject. The tyrant gets to do exactly what he chooses and rewards the subject only as long as subjugation and submission are complete.

In either case, the subject is allowed considerable freedom, except when summoned by or in the presence of the tyrant. The difference between taxidermist and autonomist is in the style of thinging. The taxidermist needs a rigidly formal symbol and ritual. The autonomist wants illusion of change. The autonomist is likely to say, in effect, "Let's do something wild and free, anything at all we want—whatever comes into *my* head.

There is a strong autonomist streak in many militant feminists. The Women's Liberation protest against thinging is legitimate in many ways. It is true that people who live by the autonomously hostile "Playboy" philosophy "thing" women as mammary and genital symbols or as members of a special group, who alternately suffer and profit from a curious and inconsistent mystique. And it is true that many men "thing" women by talking about woman drivers, shoppers, gold-diggers, or fashion addicts. Our pairing system supports the fight to break down hostile stereotyping of women. For example, our Gender Club and other exercises counteract stereotypes and double-standards.

On the other hand, such thinging is far from universally practiced today. Yet the most militant feminists shout out that they are *always* seen first as women, and therefore as inferior. We suggest that when a woman feels *continuously* thinged, it is because she things herself, causing others to treat her as a thing.

Autonomists—who are just as often male—like intense semblances of intimacy, such as sexual passion. This is often bait for them, as it was for Mark, who was passive with women. He did not have to reach out for sex, and he illuded himself that he had conquered Terry.

The realistic pairer cannot be exploited for long by the autonomist, who, while seeming to grant freedom, always asserts control. Any passionate assertion of self tends to make the autonomist flee, as Terry did when Mark made a realistic demand for change.

THE "AS-IF" RELATIONSHIP

In this relationship, one or both partners behave as if there are contracts between them that do not in fact exist. It is a way to get the privileges of intimacy without going to the trouble of actually reaching intimacy; so it exists only in illusion. The realistic pairer spots the inappropriateness of "as-if" behavior very quickly. He sees it as a manipulation and stops it by simply challenging it.

Sarah, one of our pairing trainees, reported the rudimentary example of meeting Elliot at a party. He took her home and politely opened the door lock for her. Instead of stepping back, he walked into her apartment, turned on the light and took off his coat.

"When I looked annoyed," she said, "he said, 'Well, you were going to ask me in, weren't you?' "

"In the past," Sarah added, "I would have colluded with this little illusion of his rights. I would have been afraid to offend him. Now I just shook my head, smiled politely, and helped him on with his coat."

The as-if device sometimes continues to operate much like a perpetual-motion machine, once the target of the game permits it to begin.

Edith met Patrick at an art class. Afterward they had coffee and a sandwich together. Next night he called her. "You know," he said, "there's a play on UHF television that I'm dying to see, and my set has just gone completely black. Do you suppose I could watch it at your place?"

Edith had difficulty in pairing. It was a relief to her to feel that the preliminaries were magically over, that Patrick was already something of an intimate. Her rejection anxiety was greatly eased. So she did not object as Patrick came over and made himself comfortable, putting an arm around her in a familiar way, and later following her into the kitchen to look for snacks.

Unlike Sarah in the previous case, Edith permitted this pattern, with the illusion of friendship to continue. Patrick did not hesitate to ask her for help with typing a doctoral dissertation and then with sewing some curtains. He talked over his problems with her, using her as a kind of therapist. He got her to help him shop for lampshades, and then one night, applying the same kind of presumption, he made love to her.

Edith now assumed they were real lovers. She made all his problems hers, worried about him, and did for him. Patrick was always good company and full of talk—about everything except their relationship and his feelings about her.

Edith was not very talkative. When she had problems, she did no more than state them briefly. Patrick listened, but offered little real comment, except to cluck sympathetically or to reflect—like a mirror—whatever other emotion *she* expressed: anger, worry, indignation. Since Edith was terribly uncomfortable about discussing her own feelings, she was glad not to be under any obligation to talk about anything that was unpleasant for her.

After several months, Patrick telephoned to say he had a great job offer in another state, but he would have to leave in two weeks. Edith helped him pack books and dishes, carried boxes to his station wagon, and waved him off. He wrote a note a week after he got there, describing the job, the weather, and the people. Three weeks later he sent another, much shorter note. Thereafter Edith heard nothing, except for cards on her birthday and Christmas. Crushed and disenchanted, she sought understanding in a pairing class.

There she came to realize that Patrick was another kind of segmentalist—a pairing opportunist, who was content to use her in whatever ways she was useful. He assumed that he had a right to take whatever she did not actually refuse. Had she demanded a realistic intimate exchange with him, he would almost certainly have backed away.

Patrick, she understood, was not a dyed-in-the-wool nonintimate. He was probably capable of intimacy, but he was intimacy *resistant*. He was content with taking the surface fruit of intimacy and foregoing the deeper satisfactions of tending the tree and then harvesting the full crop. Again, Edith was not just a victim. She, too, had wanted a shortcut to intimate rewards and did not want to deal with the realities of a truly intimate relationship. She was much like the naïve soul who dreams of easy money and becomes easy prey for swindlers. She could not have been taken in if she had not been doing a little taking all her own. She practiced the common fantasy that if you "make nice" and keep a relationship peaceful, love will grow.

Once Edith began to understand the joys of real intimacy, of real expression and fulfillment with another, she was protected from as-if relationships. For when a partner demands reality, an as-if pairer is either forced to take the frightening step into the waters of intimacy, or to run.

THE PAIRING HUSTLE

The pairing hustler, or con man, is a close relative to the as-if pairer. The con man is an experienced pseudointimate who practices the art of seeming to offer perfect accommodation and provides his partner with the delightful feeling: "At last, I've found the kind of partner I've *dreamed* of!" He does fit dreams amazingly. But it is time for wholesome skepticism when much that one wants comes with no effort.

Like the as-if pairer, the hustler also seeks benefits of intimacy without involving himself or committing himself to the quest for reality. But the hustler does not look for these benefits on a broad scale. He is more likely to be seeking certain specific things. And while the as-if pairer provides the illusion of a full relationship, the hustler is usually more efficient. He listens and watches carefully to learn the pairing dreams, the specific unrealistic expectations, of a partner. He then creates the illusion of satisfying them. The result is the delightful sensation of living out a dream, which is exactly what is happening.

Though the hustler sounds vicious, he usually is not. He is an intimacy-shy person, who satisfies his own pairing needs in this special way. Frequently, he recruits several partners to fill his needs, perhaps one for sex, one for companionship, one for social connections. He sees each of them segmentally, not as whole people. Like other intimacy-resistant types, he fears to be transparent lest his own presumed unworthiness become visible, and he be rejected.

Every man who met Cindy at a party declared her absolutely charming, and went home somewhat disconsolately with his own date or wife. The men who knew her better were even more enchanted, though considerably more frustrated.

Carl knew her as the perfect sex partner. She liked everything just the way he did, and seemed delighted to share all his little idiosyncrasies. Besides, she generously ignored the fact that he was a threadbare Ph.D. candidate, and could provide her with scarcely any other entertainment. But Carl was an attractive man and a good lover. He had no trouble finding sex. What really enchanted him was the way she shared his fascination with astronomy. She kept saying that she wanted to go to evening lectures with him, to help edit and type his thesis and to learn from him. Sadly, her efforts to survive as a painter, her long hours of work, and her part-time jobs had not yet permitted this. But soon—

At the same time, Larry, who owned the largest art gallery in town, appreciated Cindy's work as an assistant in preparing shows and handling customers. She was the only employee he permitted to work part time, and whose paintings he would sell. The poor girl had no time to share Larry's great passion, music. At least not just now. It was a rare thing to find an art talent who understood his feelings about music. They had many plans to attend concerts, to listen to the Ring Cycle on records of a winter weekend, but the plans remained just plans.

Meanwhile Greg looked forward to the day when Cindy and he could realize some of their plans to enjoy their mutual love of the outdoors—ski weekends, trail hikes, ice-boating. Cindy really understood his feelings about such matters. And she was an excellent hostess at the many parties he gave for the town's elite, as well a perfect companion when he was invited out.

Cindy was not consciously defrauding these three men who were providing for so many of her needs. The con man, or woman, in love is rarely guilty of vicious intent, and tends to be the victim of his own dreams. Any of the men could have stopped Cindy's game by asserting specific demands.

"Exactly when, today, are we going to—?" was the only realistic question they had to ask. Probably they sensed this, but demurred for fear of breaking a comfortable illusion. After all, they were using Cindy to supply their dream needs.

There are many levels of conning. All may be spotted through one or more of the following symptoms:

1. Failure to follow up on promises and pleasant fantasies of the future. A check-out confronta-

tion is the answer to this "Someday Syndrome."

2. Unilateral following and leading. In pairing, the lead swings back and forth. In illusive relationships, it tends to become fixed. Cindy's men placed themselves in the leader-teacher role. The consistency of her role as a follower was one of the unrealistic expectations that Cindy met for her men.

3. Failure of any resistances or reservations to appear. Men loved Cindy, because she never had complaints, demands, or awkward questions. The illusion was, "You are perfect for me."

4. Unwillingness to talk about the future of the relationship.

5. Avoiding feedback of important demands. Cindy always evaded when the man's fantasy threatened to become a real demand. She never responded directly or quite acknowledged what he said.

6. Red Cross Nursing. Encouraging of unilateral dependence, evidenced by an unending let-me-help-*you* atmosphere. (*See The Set-Up Operation*, later in this chapter.)

7. One-sidedness of opening up. "Tell me your hopes, dreams, fears, and feelings. But I won't tell you mine."

THE BED OF ROSES

This is probably the simplest unwanted relationship to recognize, and it may well be the saddest. For these are genuinely kind, loving people. They would never give one another pain through criticism, or risk making the other feel inadequate, through hard demands.

The philosophy behind the Bed of Roses is that lovers cannot be angry, that accommodations can always solve problems, and that if one only loves enough, this produces endless ability to accommodate. Furthermore, according to this false premise, one ought to be kind enough to spare one's partner any knowledge of his failures as an act of loving charity.

The Bed of Roses used to be functional in the world of Victorianism, where lovers addressed one another as Mister and Miss, communicated in *billets doux* via messages carefully copied from handbooks of love, and depended on flowers, candy, and discreet looks and movements to do the rest. The flaw of such a pairing is that it is bloodless, and completely denies any possibility of intimacy.

From the simplest cell to the most elegant meshing of organisms—the pairing of modern men and women—one rule is unvarying: where there is life, there is conflict. Where conflict is denied or barred, life withers.

When the endless accommodations of Bed-of-Roses relationships are attempted today, they lead to gunny-sacking of resentment. Then come safety valve explosions of awesome size, or steady leakage from the gunnysack that poisons the Bed of Roses with hypocrisy.

THE ISOLATION WARD

This is a broad category, and elements of it tend to appear in almost all relationships that depend upon illusion. But in the story of Gene and Molly, isolation is the main feature.

They were both twenty-seven, both junior-college graduates. both computer programmers for the same firm. There were many other similarities, and only two notable differences. Gene was exceptionally handsome, Molly rather plain. Molly was white, and Gene was black.

They talked for months as friends, on the job, in the lunchroom, at coffee breaks. Eventually, they could not fail to recognize their romantic attraction for one another. When Gene one day spilled out some of his deepest feelings about the pain of being black, the last door seemed to open. Molly took his hand, and they did not want to let go.

They began seeing each other on nights and weekends. Molly lived with her parents, and Gene lived in the ghetto area of a small New Jersey town near the plant. Gene urged Molly not to tell her parents. They would be too upset, he was sure. So they took the long bus ride to Manhattan's Greenwich Village, where black-white pairings are not unusual.

Within two months, they were familiar figures at small restaurants and coffee houses in the Village. Then a friend of Gene's who lived in the Village got a job that kept him traveling a great deal, and let them use his apartment.

Gene and Molly spent long hours in brave fantasies: *Can you imagine their faces at the plant if I walked in with your ring on my finger? I wonder if that Puerto Rican couple in accounting might not like to go out with us. Or maybe we could have a little party here at the apartment some Saturday night—you know, a simple dinner and some drinks, and each of us ask some of our less prejudiced friends. Don't you think they'd get along? After all, the world is changing. Not everyone has a small mind.*

But they never did anything about these fantasies. Molly pressed hard for a while to make their pairing public in some small way. "It just isn't fair to have to feel we're hiding something as lovely as this," she would say.

Gene, however, would always find practical objections, though he claimed not to object in theory. Then one evening, as they walked down Sixth Avenue, they met a white pair Molly had known in college. No one seemed shocked or upset, and they all decided to have dinner together.

It started out good, but it faded fast. Gene and Molly repeatedly caught themselves staring at each other. Both became quiet. This small event of reality, the first to intrude into their isolation, had tremendous impact. Simultaneously, they realized that neither had the courage to face the long-term problems of a black-white pairing. Things were never the same again. Two months later a bitter Gene left for California, leaving a chastened and shaken Molly behind.

The Isolation Ward is perhaps the most fertile of all seedbeds for illusion. For just as an individual has no contact with reality when he is isolated and becomes neurotic, so it is with a pair.

This explains much of the perennial tragedy of extramarital affairs. Often, such a relationship may be intrinsically valid and would ordinarily have a high potential for genuine, rewarding intimacy. The pairers themselves may be open and authentic with one another. Yet the required secrecy spells isolation, and that isolation will number the days of intimacy.

Extra-marital lovers may think and feel for a time

that the hide-and-seek of isolation is exciting. But it is almost impossible for extra-marital pairing to survive unless the destructive force of social isolation is counteracted.

Complete isolation is not necessary, even for extra-marital pairers. They often have more social options than they think. They tend to over-react and isolate themselves more than tact requires. Some such couples find a friend or two who maintain discretion and think the couple good company. Some find ways to involve one another openly in work or professional association, so that only the sexual aspect is unexposed.

On the other hand, extra-marital pairers should not create conflicts within people who resist such relationships. To introduce one's lover to one's grown children, for example, is a hostile use of an extra-marital affair because it can create intense conflicts of loyalty in the young people.

Isolation is sometimes used as an illusion-preserver by the pairing hustler, the taxidermist, or others who would like to manufacture a nonintimate, but binding relationship; the fake front that "Ours is a worthwhile relationship" can only survive in isolation. If an illuding couple gets a close look at some good pairings, unrealistic elements in their own relationship become apparent by comparison. In isolation, the quality of a relationship can become whatever a couple says it is.

No amount of self-assertion or open expression of feeling is enough to overcome fully the effect of isolation. Though the feelings may be genuine, the setting is so unreal that the perception of feeling is distorted.

How can the realistic pairer deal with isolation? Only by breaking out of it. If a potential intimate seeks recognition and acceptance of others, so does a pair need recognition and acceptance by others. It is a simple recognition, and often a fairly superficial one, of joint image. ("Hi, John! How's Mary?")

The *pairingness* of a couple can be confirmed only by the world around them. The proverbial lovers who want to shout their love from the rooftops really want someone to hear them. Lovers-in-hiding, runaways from reality, are silent and soon fall into depression.

When Molly and Gene, the mixed couple, met friends in Greenwich Village, each quickly read in the friend's actions and eyes: "That man is black, and that woman is white. They are in for one rough time." From that moment on, neither Molly nor Gene could hide from reality any longer.

So the wise pair does more than assert personal realities to one another. They also *assert* the reality of their pairing authentically. They appear as a pair before friends, family, business contacts—and real responses pour back. The pairer wants them because they are real. The illuder hides from them in his secret corner.

PAIRING BY POPULAR DEMAND

They were everyone's perfect pair in college days. He was the tall, powerful football hero. She was full-figured, blond, and became Homecoming Queen in a walkaway. Both were so clean-cut and bright and wholesome that everyone said they were born for each other. It was a Royal Pairing, a joining of the purple.

Both sets of parents wept when they saw what choice the young had made. For both mothers, especially, all their romantic dreams were realized. Wherever the two went, everyone looked and smiled. And in private, they would look into a mirror with toothpaste smiles before they left their castle and say, "We look really neat together, don't we?"

There are many kinds of royal pairings—of wealth, of intellect, of talent, of power. They would seem to have little in common with the Isolation Ward. Yet they produce almost exactly the same result.

The validation of the royal pairing is in the public, rather than the intimate, eye. While they hold court, perhaps as the song duo, the laboratory research team, the dancing partners, or the mixed-doubles champs, they feel real and rewarded. But when they are alone, they are not fully real people for one another. For they have turned themselves into the two component parts of One Thing: whatever brought them joint popular acclaim or recognition. And it is only with great difficulty that a person can assert his own identity privately when he depends so much on public reaction.

Royal Pairs face other special problems. Failures of any kind are incompatible with their public image and therefore cause these couples undue anxiety. Unfortunately, sexual failure is particularly common in these pairings. For sexuality gets no public approval. It is real and private.

Couples who get together because "everybody" says they are "made for each other" derive their intimacy at least in part from outside social pressure. The kicks they get from public display of popularity evaporate when the bedroom doors close at night and the couple may be confronted with an essentially empty relationship. Such failure is not only common in Hollywood, when idols fall for other idols, but whenever social approval takes the place of real intimacy.

Failure was so unacceptable in one case that the "beautiful" couple began to construct a series of illusions to excuse them from lovemaking. She decided that The Pill made her gain too much weight and spoiled her complexion. He found a magazine article suggesting that intrauterine devices might lead to various ills. She rejected the diaphragm-jelly method as mechanical and ugly. They agreed that condoms and foam were so unnatural that these methods turned them off. The result was the elimination of any acceptable birth-control method save abstinence. Sex all but stopped for this Royal Pair.

If such couples know and use pairing techniques early, they can avoid these traps. They can assert themselves as individuals and develop authentic conflicts that deny the illusion supported by outsiders. Such couples should also become consciously aware of polarities and pay attention to authentic differences.

Ed and Irene were both first-rate athletes, known to their sporting-set friends as The Champs. Their social lives centered around the athletic club. They came to the Institute because their promising love affair was becoming a constant irritant.

Once they had begun to learn reality-testing, they joined the art museum. He favored modern painting; she liked the classic sculpture. They began to take part in a local little theater, where Irene proved a natural actress, and Ed used his public-relations skill to raise money and sell tickets. They were still regarded as a couple by their friends but as their Siamese-twin image cracked, their intimacy grew.

The parent-promoted pairing—"Wouldn't our kids make a great couple at the club?"—is another troublemaker. So is the friend-sponsored pairing—"She was the prettiest girl in my class, and I know you'll love her!"

Fortunately, resistance against such innocent manipulation by friends and family is usually strong. The pair know they are being thinged, and each associates the other with the thinging. Aggressive self-assertion is their salvation, and it need not lead to rejection. The pair can express the resentment they feel, level with one another, and then rebel as a twosome.

Roy was to pick up Jean at her apartment and then take her to their sponsoring friend's boat for an all-day outing. The drive to the harbor was long, and Roy was one of our pairing students. After fifteen minutes, he admitted to himself the sullen resentment he was starting to feel. Suddenly, he stopped the car.

"Listen, Jean," he said. "I have a reservation about you. May I tell it to you?"

"What do you mean, a reservation?" she bristled.

"A negative feeling."

"That's a strange thing to tell a girl the minute you meet her," she said coldly. "But if you have to, go ahead."

"If I had met you any other way, I'd be on top of the world. You're just the sort of girl I seem to like. Jack was right, though I hate to admit it. You're pretty, bright, and I suspect you're warm when you're not being pushed at some guy. (Jean smiles involuntarily.) But if we go through a whole day of Jack and Alice watching us out of the corners of their eyes to see how it's going, and nudging us every chance they get, we'll never see each other again. We'll feel like a couple of poodles being mated.

Jean said: "I guess you're right. I was feeling uptight."

"Well, there's a phone right over there," said Roy. "I can reach Jack at the boat. Then we can go to a great little restaurant I know . . ."

"Wait a minute. Don't I have something to say about where we go?"

"Yes, but I'm asking you to go to a place I want to take us. What you decide is up to you."

Authenticity, most of our students say, is habit-forming. Once the taste is acquired, you are uncomfortable without it, and always seem able to find your way back to it.

THE SET-UP OPERATION

This style is perhaps the most subtle and variable of all. Here is a fairly simple example of it.

Allan quickly becomes quite infatuated with Barbara. But his anxiety about losing her is equally strong. She is an unusually pretty girl, who loves male attention and responds to it easily. She also likes to keep her distance. She spends many evenings at home alone, and always has an excuse if Allan suggests that he join her, so that they can both have company as they read, write letters, or watch television.

He has had great success with friends and acquaintances through his stepping in generously whenever they need any help. This has been so rewarding for him that he watches carefully and expectantly for signs of trouble, and is known for his caring attitude toward others.

"What would we have done without old Allan?" is a phrase he has heard many times.

Wanting to bond Barbara to him, he sets out to make himself useful. Barbara is several years younger than he, a little careless and casual. One evening she calls him to say that her car is stalled and asks what she ought to do. He rushes to her, finds that her car is out of gas and gets her started. Barbara is grateful. Gradually, Allan begins to take on his identity of the White Knight, the personal protector of Barbara.

Barbara, of course, does not need much rescuing. So Allan helps to create situations that call for rescue. He is a young physician, so he keeps dropping such lines as, "How long have you had that mole? It looks questionable to me." "Have you been tested for anemia lately?" He insists on days of bed rest if she has a cold. He plans her diet.

Allan also checks Barbara on the kind of insurance she buys for her car, the kind of loan she gets for a vacation, the lease on her apartment. Always he is suspicious, concerned that she will be overcharged, victimized, cheated.

Barbara is also afraid of losing Allan. And she quickly becomes aware that when she calls for rescue she invariably catches his immediate attention. So she colludes. She helps Allan set up perils for her. She asks his advice for everything, lets him shield her from the world.

Eventually Barbara becomes rather helpless. This locks the pair into their collusion. Now her needs are real and constant. But this role-playing has quite a price. For each has become a symbol, a thing, White Knight and Periled Lady. Real intimacy becomes blocked, and the stage is set for resentment to develop on both sides. Her constant needs become an irritation for him, and she is bitter about his having crippled her and put her under his constantly watchful eye.

The set-up operation has endless variations. Irene is worried about losing Leonard, because he is far better educated and more intellectual than she. She wishes to demonstrate that he lacks common sense, and that she has a practical mind. So she starts collecting bits of evidence to this effect, usually simple household matters, to which he gives little thought and she gives much.

"You didn't have to make two trips to the trash barrel," she helpfully points out. "You could have poured the stuff from all four wastebaskets into one."

Or: "Look how much extra you spend buying cigarettes from machines, instead of a carton." Before long, Leonard feels like an absent-minded professor. But he helped create the situation by enjoying Irene's interest and attention.

There is, as usual, a built-in warning sign against this trap. It is the mild annoyance one begins to feel in response to constant minor correction and interference. If it is calmly discussed, as it should be between genuine intimates, the set-up operation ceases to be rewarding to the partner who has begun it, and it stops.

THE DETECTIVE STORY

It begins because people are genuinely curious about those they love. They want an answer to the question, "What sort of person is my love in his relations with others in the world?"

So the involved pairer is entitled to watch carefully now and then, perhaps at parties—"What is he

like with other women?"—or in a visit to the office—
"How does he treat his superiors, and underlings?—
or at her house—"Is she in debt? Why that stack of
unpaid bills?"

In general, partner-watching, begins as a legitimate—indeed essential—quest for information, an
effort to gain a variety of perspectives of this very
important other person.

But such questioning may also begin to fill other
needs. The questioner may really be saying, "You
don't communicate a very full and real image of
yourself and your feelings to me, so I must find out
in any way I can." In many courting-style relationships this feeling eventually becomes very vexing
and changes to such sentiments as: "I feel you are
misleading me about where I stand with you," or "I
feel you have ulterior motives in the way you treat
me; because you hold the power of love over me,
you take advantage and exploit me."

The person who feels this way sometimes sets up
a snooping system to determine the truth or falsity
of his or her fears, or to document conclusions secretly arrived at and never directly expressed. When
natural curiosity becomes unnecessarily camou-
flaged, a supposedly intimate partner turns into a
district attorney.

SHE:
"You weren't in the office when I called today at
two."

HE:
"I had a business lunch."

SHE:
"Your secretary said she didn't see a business lunch

on your calendar. That's why I called three times; she said you should be in any minute."

HE:

"I'm sorry. I ran into a guy I know from Webster Company, and we had lunch together. He had a great idea about—"

SHE:

"Your secretary said a man from Webster had called you six times, too, that I wasn't the only one . . ."

HE:

"That was Charlie's partner. It was quite a coincidence, running into Charlie—Fate, almost—and . . ."

SHE:

"Yes, wasn't it! Does Charlie have long brown hair? I'm only teasing of course. But look what's on the back of your jacket."

The partner-detective seems always to be collecting evidence for a trial, always quizzing as if trying to prove a case. For example:

SHE:

"You've burned two tiny holes in this lovely new shirt, dear. Are you really cutting down your smoking? You know how it worries me."

HE:

"Oh, sure I'm cutting it down."

SHE:

"Your fingers still have such tobacco stains. You must still be smoking a lot when you're under pressure. Why don't you let me carry your cigarettes for you tonight, and you can ask me whenever you want one."

HE (trying to be light about it):
"They're not too heavy ..."

SHE:
"Well, then let me have the matches. I read an article that said going without matches is a good way to make yourself aware of how much you smoke. I think you smoke much more than you realize. Here. I'll count your cigarettes now. It's one o'clock. Let's see how long ..."

The case that is being developed here is that he is not fully aware and responsible. This young woman is really saying, "I don't trust you because you don't reveal yourself to me. I'm trying to let you know that I know. I'm also trying to suggest that *you* can't really trust *yourself*. If you'll admit it, I'll be less afraid of the power you have in our relationship. I feel this way because I don't seem able to have *impact* on you."

In an open relationship, such spirals of suspicion cannot develop. When relationships are covert and partners convey the feeling that they are keeping a lot of intimate information secret, the other person may respond by trying to get some sort of control, i.e., impact power.

The lady who wants to control her man's matches is saying, "Hey, I'm a person. You can tell that because you have to ask me for a match if you want to smoke, and I may then try to stop you. I will then feel like part of your life, rather than a thing you use for some purpose that you won't talk about."

Spying is meant to convey the same message: "I am a person. You can tell. because I know things about you, maybe more than even you know. You may as well tell me the rest."

The Detective Story stops, like all detective stories, as soon as the mystery is solved. In intimate relationships, the mystery is, "Who and what are you as a person? What am I to you? Where are we heading? I must know, because you are important to me, and without this information, I cannot trust you."

No spying is needed once the secretive partner levels, becomes transparent, and thereby trustworthy.

THE GUILT AND THE OBLIGATION FACTORY

Guilt is a powerful factor in human relationships, and can be most difficult even for therapists to handle. But the pairing system can often eliminate it. Why?

When you feel guilty about a relationship, you accept responsibility for what happens to the other person. The classic psychoanalyst's answer is, "You are both adults. Each of you has responsibility for himself. You made a choice. They made a choice. You can't be responsible for any choice but your own."

It seems a reasonable point of view, but it does not reflect the facts. When people do not have an open relationship they are guilty of concealment, and they feel it. When something goes wrong, that feeling emerges as, "I tricked him or her. He or she couldn't tell what they were getting into because I deceived."

This feeling is strong in a nonintimate relationship because it is so true. Each person feels that the other might have acted differently, if they had been in possession of the facts. But facts were hidden, and the partner who suppressed information under the courting system feels that he unduly influenced the other's decisions and is responsible for his actions.

The partner who uses the pairing system and promptly opens his feelings, is much less susceptible to guilt. If something goes wrong, he may be very unhappy and feel great sympathy for his partner. But he does not feel guilty.

The guilt factory that is established by many couples can become perversely rewarding. Making one's partner feel guilt is easy to do. It is a potent way to manipulate, to control, and bind someone to oneself. The proverbial Jewish Mother—who can just as easily be the Catholic Mother or the Buddhist Mother—is a monument to this style of conducting intimate business, but the style is just as common among younger singles.

Paula and Dick return from an all-day date.

DICK:
May I come up and say goodnight?

PAULA:
No, Dick. Not tonight.

DICK:
But it's early. What's wrong? I'll behave. I won't throw you onto the bed [he jokes] unless you insist.

PAULA (the suggestion of sexual exploitation makes her gunnysack of stored-up resentments spill over):
Don't you care anything about how I feel? Do you just need sex and don't care about anything else? You've insisted on your way all day without a single thought about my feelings!

DICK (shocked):
I thought we had a fine day. What do you mean?

PAIRING

PAULA:

Any considerate person would have known I spent two hours on my hair. They wouldn't have put the top down. But what could I say, unless I wanted to look like a bad sport? Did I say a word when you insisted on going to the races as a surprise? You had the tickets, so how could I say I hated the races and those disgusting wooden seats? Did I tell you that noisy bar gave me a headache? Did I bitch about making do with those awful fish snacks at that party you dragged me to, instead of taking me out to dinner?

Poor Dick. What can he say? What did he know? At once he takes on a placating manner. He begins to make promises. He tells Paula how much he feels for her, exaggerating more and more, as if to compensate for "errors" that she could easily have prevented but chose to let him commit so that he could hang himself and be at her mercy. She has now convinced him that he is a boor, insensitive to the needs and wishes of others.

Paula is not inventing her list of gripes. It is real. But it comes a bit late. She is making a series of demands for change. But they are demands to change the past, which is an impossibility. Dick would like to change, but he cannot make the changes that Paula demands and therefore feels frustration and guilt. All he can do is "make up" for the injuries that he unwittingly inflicted. The stage is now set for Paula to ask almost anything of him, and it would be difficult for him to resist without making himself feel even guiltier.

Deep psychological complexities are at work here. For Paula masochistically accepts misery in such situations, almost enjoys it. Why? While she suffers, she is like a man digging a ditch, miserable with fatigue, but knowing that he is working on overtime and that every minute is building his paycheck rapidly. With her discomfort Paula was buying control over Dick.

How people learn this kind of behavior from infancy is a psychanalytic problem. We deal with it on a here-and-now basis. First, one must recognize guilt manipulation. Its distinguishing characteristic is the demand for impossible change, such as changing the past.

One can then put the guilt and obligation factory out of business, not by labeling or mind-reading the other's secret motivations—which may well be unconscious—but by stating one's own real feelings, revealed by knowledge and a moment's meditation.

Dick might say, "Paula, I'm sorry the day was unpleasant for you, because I enjoyed it. You were a good companion. You make me wish I could start all over again. But I can't. The awful thing is, I feel guilty now, and that makes me do one thing I really don't want to do—resent the fact that I didn't know you were uncomfortable. I like you too much to want to resent you and spoil our relationship. And I want you to know that I would always try to make any change I could—if you would just tell me when something is wrong."

If Paula is a deep-dyed guilt manipulator, it may take a long time for her to change. But Dick has at least let her know that he will not play the guilt game. If he really does respond to her wishes, without himself accommodating so much that *he* becomes secretly miserable, she may learn that straightforward, *immediate* expression of her feelings is more rewarding than manipulation.

The guilt manipulator often has a strong nonintimate streak, as do all manipulators. This represents anxiety, a fear about being used, or controlled. But the building of genuine trust, and the experience of expressing feelings genuinely without losing love, eventually make the business of guilt-manufacturing unnecessary.

18

Some
special problems
of pairing

THE varieties and vagaries of human love are virtually infinite. We cannot hope to explain them all. For example, some of the people who are served at the Institute are homosexual. But while we find that homosexual pairings can be guided toward intimacy, we cannot explore the problems and the methods here.

We believe, however, that the vast majority of pairing problems are amenable to the sensitive and intelligent application of the intimate principles we have discussed. For example, one reason for the tendency toward rapid breakdown of homosexual relationships is plainly the *isolation* that characterizes them, the secrecy required in a rather intolerant heterosexual society. We have discussed why isolation is destructive and what must be done about it. The imaginative reader can proceed from these principles to his own special case.

To help the reader understand the pattern of making such extensions, we will cite a few special questions that have been asked of Dr. Bach by pairers and will show how the general rules apply.

QUESTION:

Dr. Bach, whenever Laura visits my apartment, she loves to wash any dirty dishes, mend things, and make arrangement of flowers and greens she brings. Sometimes she arrives with whole pies or cakes she's baked for my sweet tooth. It always makes me a little uncomfortable. I don't do anything personal for her. She gets upset if I even try to pay for ingredients. What's more, I really like sex with her a lot, and she admits that while she likes it, it's not nearly so important to her. How can I keep my accounts in balance?

DR. BACH:

The fact that you raise the question of "accounts" suggests that you are making a basic pairing error. Laura is plainly expressing her feelings in her own way. You must respect those feelings and not try to stifle their expression, not try to force Laura to express herself in *your* terms, which would be insisting that she accommodate to you and would tend to breed resentment. It is a simple truth of pairing that one partner gives more than the other. The giver and the receiver may change roles at any time. But neither should feel either indebted or used. Each gives in his own way, of his own special abilities, and emotional accounting is impossible. The debts of love can never be paid.

QUESTION:

I see Marian two or three times a week. In between, I think of her endlessly. I daydream about how she looks, and how it is to touch her. I feel a great deal for her. But then, when I call for her, the crazy thing is, I feel like a stranger. Marian says she has the same reactions. It takes an hour or more before we begin to see each other as intimates again. Are we kidding ourselves in some way about what our relationship really is? If not, what's wrong?

DR. BACH:

Really, probably nothing is wrong. You are only dealing with the "re-entry problem." Unless a pairing is of the "continuous" type—in marriage, or living together, characterized by a constent flow of information about the activities and thoughts of the other—re-entry must be managed after each separation. During that separation, the lives of the pair diverge, and especially in the early phases of the relationship, the couple in effect become strangers again. The longer the separation, the more fantasized and perhaps idealized become their images of one another. In a sense, in re-entering each other's lives, they must go through a re-introduction. To do this quickly, they should apply the principles of instant intimacy and seek to have aggressive impact upon one another.

QUESTION:

What is the best way to handle such reintroductions?

DR. BACH:

The principles are similar to those of a first meeting, modified by the obvious fact that you know one another. First, be sure to go through some ceremony of greeting, of recognizing one another. "Gosh, it's hot," is not a greeting ceremony. "It's good to see you again," is more to the point. The sense of being strangers derives in large part from separation anxiety. A reminder of your closeness is important, even if it is only a book she has been wanting to borrow, or remembering that she likes strawberry ice cream. Since anxiety is further reduced by the expression of real feelings, including real reservations, a little catching up on your own degree of involvement is advisable. Keep the conversational attention on the pairing, not on the new county budget or world affairs. You can intensify the re-entry warm-up by bringing up unresolved hurts from the last meeting and trying to resolve them.

QUESTION:
Would making love ease the re-entry?

DR. BACH:
It may. Such sex seems to yield strong emotional reassurance, but to be erotically unimaginative and quick. On the other hand, sex between such pairers at parting seems to incorporate a powerful impact, an attempt to bind before leaving. Many pairers report that parting sex seems to be unusually exciting and fulfilling. But in cases in which the parting brings excessive anxiety, the tension seems to distract and minimize the sexual expression. When the separation anxiety becomes great enough, it often leads to conflict and hostility as leaving grows near. The pairer should not be quick to make too much of such conflicts, for they tend to make angry mountains out of emotional molehills. Actually these trumped-up battles unconsciously help lovers to part.

QUESTION:
For some reason I'm not sure I understand, I seem to keep falling in love with two men at the same

time. I think I have real intimacy with both just now. One of them agrees. The other says this idea is impossible, that I must be shallow. Many of my friends are very critical; some even imply that I am promiscuous. Can I pair authentically with more than one person?

DR. BACH:
Authentic multiple pairing is possible, but extremely ambitious and energy-demanding, with a high risk of complicating love until it becomes chaotic and eventually superficial. The ability to pair-multiply is rare, but it may be checked out with the following test:

1. Can you sustain more than one sexual relationship, with satisfaction for both yourself and the respective partners?
2. Does a second sexual relationship provide carry-over stimulation for the first, and vice versa, enhancing both relationships—not diminishing either of them?
3. Can you free yourself and your partners from jealousy, competitive comparisons, and possessiveness?
4. Is it stimulating—and not confusing—to have different aspects of your personality drawn into play for each partner?
5. Can you openly assert your preference for multiple pairing with both partners, without guilt or deception, without becoming a multiple cheat?
6. Are you sure you are not using multiple pairing to dilute each involvement and thus evade any true intimacy?
7. Are you sure you are not confusing multiple

pairing with a more primitive desire for sexual variety?
8. Do you have the time, money, energy, planning skills, and independence of social approval to manage the inherent complexities of multiple relationships?

Unless you can honestly answer six of these eight questions with a genuine and unqualified *yes*, we recommend that you reconsider your interest in multiple pairing. However, if you can respond affirmatively, there is nothing in our pairing principles that stands in the way of achieving multiple intimacy.

19

The end—
or the
beginning

POETS to the contrary, there is nothing very sweet about parting from love. If you still love, but are separated by circumstance or by the withdrawal of your partner, it hurts. You will survive, and you know it, but the pain is no less acute.

If you no longer love or want to keep a love, the parting should be far less painful and upsetting. Under the courting system, this is often not the fact. Good pairers can make a cleaner break.

Love's end starts at its beginning, as does life itself. How does one enter love? If it is with an unrealistic expectation, the love may die, but the powerful dream continues. One fights to preserve the dream, the illusion. It is hard to give up the flower-covered cottage, those four adorable children, the beautiful furnishings the two dreamers are going to have and to hold forever, along with the promise of a secure love to grant relief from all anxieties of loneliness for the rest of life.

For some courters, a whole Forsythe Saga falls

apart when a relationship comes to an end. And the dream dies hard.

The unrealistic expectations of the courter, and the habit of avoiding anxieties by fabricating illusions, are likely to make him deny the failure of love when it happens. For that failure is very rarely a dramatic event. Typically, it is a gradual waning, like the yellowing of an autumn leaf.

When the end comes subtly, it is not difficult for dreamers to deny it, sometimes even for years. By the time many courting affairs actually break up, good will has been gone and love dead for quite a while. When the couple can finally accept this, they are enormously relieved. For they are probably still genuinely fond of the old love, and cannot bear to do the partner what might be grievous injury. They cannot know what the hurt will be, because they dare not ask. And since they have not leveled along the way, they tend to assume that the partner imagines all is still as it was. Withdrawal appears to these lovers as a sudden knife cut. *All seemed fine to him today, and tomorrow I will have to tell him it is over. I cannot do it.*

How does pairing help to deal with the problem of love ending?

First, the pairer realistically enters all relationships with much the same expectation. "I want to get to know this person. I hope to be able to relate to him and to have him know me. I want to share with him what we can. The door of possibility is open. But the only demand I make is authenticity for both of us."

So the pairer is in a frame of mind to accept limitations. And from the beginning reservations are openly stated. He knows that she does not really endorse his position as a Republican Party functionary. She knows that he is sometimes driven to the brink of rage by some of her very liberated friends.

The *state-of-the-union message* is an important part of their relationship. They know where they stand with each other. We encourage pairers to ask, at regular intervals, the question, "Where are we now?" and to answer it honestly. Such encounters are not only stimulating and informative. They also make sudden reversals unlikely. Unpleasant surprises are not kept back for some sudden future moment that is constantly put off out of fear. The state-of-the-union message keeps the relationship up to date. It is something like a medical check-up.

"Listen," he may say to her, "for an evening on the town, or for an academic lecture that would put most women I know to sleep, you're the greatest company I have ever known. But, dear, please don't ask to go to the beach with me again. I just can't listen to so many worries about sunburns and what the water will do to your hair and how we'll have to leave at noon to beat the Sunday traffic. I finally know that it's possible for you to bug me."

It may sound cruel. But it avoids a crueler kind of deception later on. It eliminates false expectations on her part that he will ask her to go on his frequent seashore expeditions. She, on the other hand, may tell him that she will never again try to take him with her to shop for anything:

"I just don't like to buy until I know what's available, and what the best value is, and I can see that drives you crazy. You just want to put your money down and have it over with."

To keep current with the state of the unions, pairers can also keep a *pairing log*. Most of our students keep such a log in their heads, although some put them in writing for their own reference only. Each pair develops its own pairing history, and much understanding can be gained from keeping this history up to date and referring to it in order to recall changes that have taken place in the relationship (frequency of meetings, quality of sexual satisfaction, etc.).

Entries can encourage action based on comparisons with the past. For instance: "Again enjoyed seeing movie together with B., but she did not bubble as much in the discussion afterward. Do I inhibit her thoughts and sharing? Must check this out."

By this process, a pair can learn much about their real limitations. And by dealing with each situation honestly, as it occurs, they can maintain good will. There is no attempt to pretend perfect compatibility. What they like and share is not hidden by anxious illusions about existing differences. And if there is, in fact, little basis for a relationship, such forthrightness helps pairers to learn the facts as early as possible.

Most pairers can see the end coming. And when they feel it, they are able to say so, hard as it may sometimes seem. We will not illude the reader. Usually one partner sees the situation as more worth preserving than the other. And if a rival has pushed one out of the picture, even the most realistic person is bound to take it ill. It is a painful experience, a trauma but not a catastrophe.

Some gentle preparation is possible for an about-to-be-dropped pairer during the period we call *settling*. During this beginning-of-the-end, conflict and change are allowed to drain out of the pairing. The relationship provides little emotional stimulus and slowly becomes less desirable to the more loving partner.

Is this deception? Not really. Feelings are still

being expressed regularly, and they have tended automatically to decline in positive emotional content. Feelings that are still strong enough to trouble with become fewer and further between. The rest is tact.

Tact might be defined as honesty without cruelty. If John and Mary have been pairing for some time, John does not announce exuberantly, "Say, you'll never guess where I spent the weekend! I've just met the greatest girl in the world, and in an hour we were making wild love!"

It is almost impossible to teach tact, but good relationships are impossible without it. Conversational impulses can be censored without concealing important information. Reasonable discretion and kindness should determine what is said and what is not.

To help our students learn how to say good-bye without cruelty, we tell them right from the start why it is so important to meet without fear in the first place. The philosophy is: "If I have respected your feelings in our time together, it is unlikely that you will wish to punish me when we part."

Much of this book has been about beginnings, very little about ends. The reader may ask: what of the middle?

There really is none.

The beauty and deepest reward of pairing is that it is virtually all beginning, all becoming. There are constant resolutions, some small, some vast, some dictated by changes imposed from within the relationship, some from outside circumstances. Students become professors, masters become slaves, dependents become independents, breadwinners get fired from their jobs, the lonely become popular, wives become mothers, inhibited pairers become passionate. The list is infinite. So are growth and change.

Pairing prepares men and women to accept uncertainty, to welcome it, for uncertainty is part of life itself. Much of our effort is to teach this, to free people from the placid monotony of illusion so that they may take in the color and profusion of change. And not alone.

Glossary

SOME PAIRING DEFINITIONS

Accommodation. Adapting one's behavior so as to conform to one's partner's preconceptions of lovability, while suppressing one's own wishes and feelings, thus producing surface impressions of nonconflict.

Agape. The caring aspect of love.

Aggression, I-Type. Impact aggression; the passionate assertion of one's true desire for improving the pairing. Effective impacting on a partner is the way of gauging one's importance to a partner. Impact aggression is loaded with rational, pair-relevant information.

Aggression, H-Type. Hostile aggression; an angry reaction to the frustrations produced by pairing problems, with the intent to injure, hurt, insult, reduce.

Autonomy Worship. A currently fashionable rationalization of nonintimacy, which in effect holds that one ought not to be much changed or governed by a relationship with any other, and should just do one's "own thing."

All-Electric Meeting. A powerful but accidental impact (often nonverbal) of new partners upon one another at first meeting, resulting in maximum attraction with physiosexual response; usually called "love at first sight."

Balance. A state of optimal balance for which it is assumed pairing partners will strive, despite the frequent conflicts between opposing interests generated by the two partners. This striving to overcome the conflicts that characterize authentic pairing is emotionally involving, creatively challenging, and facilitates the growth of intimacy. The striving for "optimal distance" is a prototype for a balanced state (see *Distancing*).

Belt Line. The limit of hurt-tolerance below which partners cannot absorb blows or hurts without serious injury to the relationship. The pairing system teaches intimates to define clearly, to expose (rather than hide), and to respect contractually their Achilles' heels or beltlines and to adjust them if too high or too low. Hitting below a known beltline is a prototype of H-Type, or Hostile, Aggression.

Collusion. Cooperation with one's partner's pairing illusions; a joint denial of threatening realities; going along with something one does not really believe in.

Conflict. A more or less constant state of realistic tension in pairing, which, when accepted and worked through with constructive aggression, yields intimacy.

Contract. An arbitrary agreement restricting spontaneity of intimacy, with mostly alienating effects, except when dealing with limits or beltlines.

Courting Ethic. The traditional ethic of typical male-female relationships; a mystique of formal etiquette, accommodation, and myths supported by illusions, and aimed at creating a false ideal of intimacy without conflict; the culture-prescribed technique for dealing with universal courtship anxieties.

Dissonance. A disparity between actual behavior, style, or values and those expected by the preconceived love-frame of the partner.

Distancing. Approach or withdrawal to a comfortable degree of intimacy; avoiding both engulfment and isolation. This degree is called the "optimal distance."

Electricity. The attraction aspect of love.

Feedback. Recognizing and repeating one's partner's requests for change, or his efforts to have impact upon one.

Fire. An analogistic reference to the intimate tension system that develops between two pairing partners. As a fire at different times needs fueling, banking, or fanning to keep it going and/or under control, so does the level of intimate tension in pairing require more or less constant sensitivity and awareness.

Gender Club. Statements of stereotypes of the role and characteristics, both positive and negative, of the opposite sex; a revealing way to gain insight into pairing attitudes and prejudices.

Gunny-Sacking. Storing up unexpressed pairing resentment.

Illuding. Creating an adaptive illusion in one's own mind or the mind of a partner, an act usually determined unconsciously.

Illusion. A false perception of reality.

Imaging. Presenting what one believes will be a rejection-proof impression of oneself, either by illuding or by symbolizing oneself. Imaging is based on unilateral, self-generated projections and attributions, which, when reality-tested and checked out with the partner, frequently prove false.

Impacting. Successfully asserting one's wishes, feelings, or identity to a pairing partner. A stimulus for change.

Instant Intimacy. A style of open communication that produces immediate authentic interest between oneself and a partner, by reducing rejection anxieties, permitting mutual impact and maximizing attractive polarities and differences, leading rapidly to commitment and involvement.

Intimacy. A relationship characterized by the transparency, authenticity, and immediacy of interaction of the partners, in which each permits the other the experience and expression of his feelings; thus, essentially a relationship of trust and sharing, without fear of dealing openly with conflict.

Intimate Revolution. The rebellion against alienation and against the nonintimacy of the traditional courting ethic. The active search for new ways of developing meaningful love relationships.

Leveling. Transparent, authentic, and explicit expressions about how one truly feels in an intimate relationship, especially concerning the more conflictive or hurtful aspects; sharing the "rough edges"; a two-way intimate dialogue essential for the location of conflict areas.

Love-Frame. A rigid preconception of lovability characteristics.

Matching. A myth-supported and nonauthentic means of reducing pairing anxiety by seeking out and emphasizing similarities of a pair in background, style, and preferences.

Meditation. Focusing one's attention for the best possible perception of one's own feelings, before expressing or acting them out.

Mind-Reading. Making assumptions about the thoughts or feelings of another without checking them out with the other person.

Mind-Raping. Telling a partner what he thinks or feels, or what he *ought* to think or feel. Ignoring or even over-riding what the partner actually thinks and feels.

Molding. Transverbally expressing to a partner what one would like him to be in relation to oneself by creating a "living sculpture."

Pairing System. Principles of personal communication that facilitate realistic and authentic ways in which men and women can develop intimate relationships.

Pairing Log. Keeping track of the development of a relationship, often helpful in determining potentials or problem areas.

Polarity. A dynamic difference, either attractive or unattractive, between partners that helps to enhance their interest in one another as people, e.g. male-female, strong-weak, young-old, cross-cultural, etc.

Quadrilog. A four-voiced dialogue representing the differences between genuine feelings and expressed feelings of a pair.

Rejection Ritual. A ritual designed to reduce rejection fears and permit openness.

Reservations. Candid sharing of negative feelings about a partner or about seeming limitations of the intimacy potential of a specific pair.

Role-Bound. Limiting one's behavior to selective sex-symbol acting, in terms of preconceived roles (as of doctor, mother, seducer).

Role-Reversal. Desirable ability to put oneself in the partner's place, especially during pairing conflicts.

Segmentalizing. Seeing or treating another in terms of one narrow aspect or specific role, e.g. as sex partner or provider, rather than as a whole person (see *Role-Bound*).

Smoothing. Anxious suppression of conflicts and differences between partners to create the illusion of peace and happiness, usually by accommodation and collusion.

State-of-the-union Message. Regular review by a pair of where they stand with one another, of attractions, reservations, conflicts, joy, and so on.

Tension. The feeling of emotional interdependence that evolves in intimate pairing as each partner's action instigates a reaction, which can be either attraction or repulsion, or a mixture of both. Pairing partners can powerfully affect the level of emotional tension—both pleasant and unpleasant—between them. The rise and fall of orgastic tension during intercourse is a prototype. The pairing system encourages the optimal level of tensions.

Thinging. Treating another (or oneself) as if the person is only an object, machine, role, or symbol. A dehumanizing result of segmentalizing.

Valency. The bonding capacity of pairers to draw each other to each other.

Bibliography

Bach, George R. *Young Children's Aggressive Play Fantasies*. Psychological Monographs, Vol. 59, No. 272. Washington: 1945.

———. "Father Fantasies and Father Typing in Father-Separated Children," *Child Development*, vol. 17 (1946), pp. 63–80.

———. *Intensive Group Psychotherapy*. New York: Ronald Press, 1954.

———. *Sex and Aggression*. Tape Cassette. Chicago: Instructional Dynamics, Inc., 1970.

Bach, George R. and Bach, Roger C. F. *Foeing, Constructive Aggression in Ill Will Confrontations*. Unpublished manuscript, 1970.

Bach, George R. and Hart, Lewis. *Natural Language Indexing by Means of Data-Processing Machines*. Santa Monica: System Developing Corp., 1959.

Bach, George R. and Hart, Lewis. *Permutation Indexing of the Language of Dreams*. Santa Monica: System Developing Corp., 1960.

Bach, George R. and Hurley, John, ed. *Murder is a Family Affair*, Book manuscript, to be published 1971.
Will include Dr. Wilfred Rasch's research on the murder of the parting partner.

Bach, George R. and Pratt, P. *Swinging versus Mul-*

tiple Pairing: A Comparison of Two Forms of Multiple Sex. Journal of Sex Research, to be published 1971.

Bach, George R. and Wessel, D. "Sound Gestures of Aggression and Love—A Voice Choral Composition." Tape recorded 1970, Michigan State University. Unpublished.

Bach, George R. and Wyden, Peter. *The Intimate Enemy.* New York: William Morrow, 1969.

Berne, Eric. *Games People Play.* New York: Grove Press, 1964.

Berscheid, Ellen and Walster, Elaine Hatfield. *Interpersonal Attraction.* Reading, Mass., Addison Wesley, 1969.

Birdwhistell, Ray. *Kinesis and Context.* Philadelphia: University of Pennsylvania Press, 1969.

Davis, Flora. "The Way We Speak 'Body-Language' A Kineticist Demonstrates Body Talk." *New York Times Magazine,* May 31, 1970.
A popular, illustrated summary of Dr. Ray Birdwhistell's "body talk."

Deutsch, Ronald M. *The Key to Feminine Response in Marriage.* New York : Random House, 1968.

Ellis, Albert and Conway, Roger O. *The Art of Erotic Seduction.* New York: Lyle Stuart, Inc., 1967.

English, O. Spurgeon: A Note on the Psychotherapeutic value of an Affair, *Voices,* vol. 3 (1967), pp. 9–13.

Erikson, Eric H. *Childhood and Society* (II). Rev. ed. New York: W. W. Norton, 1964.

Fast, Julius. *Body Language.* New York: M. Evans, 1970.

Festinger, Leon. *Theory of Cognitive Dissonance.* (Stanford: Stanford University Press, 1957.

Fromm, Erich. *The Art of Loving: An Enquiry into*

the Nature of Love. New York: Harper & Row, 1956.

Glasser, William. *Reality Therapy: A New Approach to Psychiatry*. New York: Harper & Row, 1965.

Goffman, Erving. *Behavior in Public Places, Notes on the Social Organizations of Gatherings*. Glencoe: Free Press, 1963.

Heider, Fritz. "On Lewin's Methods and Theory," *Journal of Social Issues*, no. 13 (1959).

Howard, Jane. *Please Touch—A Guided Tour of the Human Potential Movement*. New York: McGraw-Hill Book Company, 1970.

Jones, Edward E. *Ingratiation: A Social Psychological Analysis*. New York: Appleton-Century-Crofts, Inc. 1964.

Laing, Ronald D. *Self and Others*. New York: Pantheon, 1970.

Lewin, Kurt. *Field Theory in Social Science: Selected Theoretical Papers*. D. Cartwright, ed. New York: Harper & Row, 1951.

_____. *Resolving Social Conflicts*. New York: Harper & Brothers, 1948. See also Marrow, A. J., 1969.

Lewin, Kurt. "The Background of Conflict in Marriage." In *Modern Marriage*, edited by M. Jung, pp. 52–69. New York: Cross, 1940.
Tension usually connotes painful stress. But Lewin meant by it a highly desirable state of mobilized energy which stimulates goal-oriented action. In pairing, the goal is the joy of true intimacy. Pairing tensions are desirably heightened by conflict, reservations (barriers), polarities, and aggressive leveling. See also the Glossary in this book.

Lorenz, Konrad. *On Aggression*. New York: Harcourt, Brace and World, 1963.

Marrow, A. J. *The Practical Theorist: The Life and*

Works of Kurt Lewin. New York: Basic Books, 1969.

Kurt Lewin and his field theory provide the theoretical bases for the pairing system. Crucial are the concepts of *interdependence and the theory of psychological tension.*

Maslow, Abraham H. *Towards a Psychology of Being.* 2nd ed. New York: Van Nostrand Reinhold, 1968.

Masters, William H. and Johnson, Virginia E. *Human Sexual Inadequacy.* Boston: Little, Brown & Co., 1970.

May, Rollo. *Love and Will.* New York: W. W. Norton, 1969.

This otherwise profound and thorough existential analysis of love fails to clarify the paradoxical love-stimulating functions of aggression because, while May proposes the reasonable juxtaposition of apathy versus love, he nevertheless perpetuates the conventional opposition of hate and love, e.g. (p. 334.) "... it is sometimes very hard to tell whether hatred *masks* love or the reverse." May also perpetuates an old myth—sanctioned by Freud—by likening fulfilling sexual orgasm to (p. 103.) "surrender" and "dying." In pairing, orgasm is experienced as rejuvenating.

Mead, Margaret. *Culture and Commitment.* New York: Doubleday & Co., 1970.

Moreno, J. L. *Who Shall Survive: Foundations of Sociometry, Group Psychotherapy and Sociodrama.* New York: Beacon House, 1934.

Packard, Vance. *The Sexual Wilderness.* New York: McKay, 1968.

Plato. *The Portable Plato.* New York: Viking Press, 1948.

Reuben, David. *Everything You Always Wanted to*

Know About Sex but Were Afraid to Ask. New York: McKay, 1969.

Satir, Virginia. "Time-Limited Intimacy," a private conversation, Chicago, 1970. Untaped and unpublished.

Schutz, William C. *Joy: Expanding Human Awareness*. New York: Grove Press, 1967.
Contains many good transverbal games and exercises helpful to the development of intimacy.

Stoller, Frederick H. "A Memorial Bibliography," assembled by William Fawcett Hill. *Comparative Group Studies*. Beverly Hills: 1970.

Symonds, Carolyn. *Sexual Mate Swappers*. Unpublished thesis in sociology. University of California at Riverside, 1970.

Storr, Anthony. *Human Aggression*. New York: Atheneum, 1968.

Walster, Elaine, (*See Berscheid*).

Wolpe, Joseph. *The Practice of Behaviour Therapy*. New York: Pergamon Press, 1969.

Appendix

Notes on Chapter 1

EVIDENCE FOR THE INTIMATE REVOLUTION

THE most convincing evidence that an ever-growing number of informed, intelligent adults (both young and older) are engaged in a serious escape from the isolation of the psychological Ice Age is their whole-hearted participation in the human potential movement. We have been very close to this movement since its inception at the Esalen Growth Center in Big Sur Hot Springs on the California coast. We have developed many of the encounter-group programs for Esalen and other growth centers. For example, with the late Dr. Fred Stoller we introduced the original "marathon," which has become the standard core program at many growth centers.

The New York Times estimates "the human potential movement may reach millions of persons before this century is over." Our experiences at the Institute of Group Therapy, in Beverly Hills, California, as consultant and program leader at many other growth centers, and as a teacher of large classes at U.C.L.A., Berkeley, Michigan State University, and elsewhere reveal an active striving for new values and new styles of living, rather than the role-bound etiquette of yesteryear. We have labeled this striving for the new ethic and the departure from old emotionally suppressive *mores* THE *INTIMATE* REVOLUTION because people seek to escape from alienation and reach for intimacy.

PAIRING BEHAVIOR IN PUBLIC

Implied and explicit courting requirements in various social settings tend to restrict, rather than facilitate, the kind of pairing exercises recommended in this book. Erving Goffman's observations in his *Behavior in Public Places* report the kind of social regulation of mutual-involvements that tend to make pairing difficult. We question the wisdom of obeying traditional "social regulations" that keep strangers of the opposite sex apart.

One rather extreme form of revolt against oppressive social conventions is a marked increase in adult participation in social situations that facilitate the participant-observations of sexual intimacies, e.g. during proceedings sponsored by private "swinger" clubs. Partners who semipublicly copulate do not thereby learn how to pair. (See Bach and Pratt, Bibliography). Our point is that the intimacy-isolation etiquette needs to be radically overhauled—not necessarily to facilitate sex orgies but to prevent embarrassments and restrictions of the getting-acquainted process of strangers meeting in public places. Where else do strangers meet? Adult singles deserve an open etiquette that refrains from downgrading their wish to get to know and to touch one another wherever they may meet.

Notes on Chapter 2

BASIC HYPOTHESES OF THE PAIRING SYSTEM

Psychologically man is not a soloist. He lives and grows best in concert with growth-furthering others. Self-sufficiency, the capability to derive meaning and fulfillment solely from within autonomy, is at best a practically necessary defense against growth-stunting states such as exploitation, over-dependency, isolation, and furnishes self-protection against pathogenic environments and people (crazy-makers). At best, autonomous periods are voluntary refueling retreats from the demands of interpersonal contact, allowing for reflective and perspective dreams, plannings, studying, recuperative sleep, and other self-maintenance functions.

However, man's most coveted state is not autonomy but *interdependence* with one or more growth-stimulating others. The most joyful growth-stimulating state we call intimacy. Highly valued experiences in genuine interpersonal intimacy include the following: complete trust; validation of one's real impact on the world; constant stimulation to move toward new experiences (change); the experience of being of weighty significance in the personal life and growth of others; periods of transcendence from concern with self through devoted caring (agape) for and facilitating the other's well-being, periods of emotional and physical warmth, and closeness associated with an emergent state of belonging; freedom from role-bound segmentation; vicarious fulfillments through co-enjoying the shared joys of others; and deepening one's comprehension of human suffering through co-pathic "vibrating" with the shared suffering of others.

The pairing system was developed to assist people in their quest for intimacy. For—as in all other areas of important human wants—there are constructive and counterproductive ways of reaching fulfillment. Many cultural, economic, sociological, and psychological factors beyond an individual's control tend to impede man's quest for intimacy. However, more often than not the individual intimacy-searcher makes this important quest more difficult for himself than he needs to. He may, for example, try to fool himself by entertaining various intimate illusions with or without the aid of drugs; he may become tired of the arduous intimacy quest and cynically settle for pseudointimacy, or he may be an autonomy worshiper. The difficulties of achieving true intimacy are also compounded by misleading, irrational guidelines to love, such as the conventional etiquette of romantic courtship.

Our pairing trainees stop avoiding and start accepting the nature of the learning tasks required to achieve intimacy. For intimacy, while highly desired, is not naturally given. It has to be learned and earned in the course of living. Further, intimacy is not only a set of feelings that deeply involve individuals; it is also, and more characteristically, a *state of union* between individuals. This state (of intimacy) the "WE" state (we call it the "fire" in the text) has qualities and properties beyond the feelings generated by the I and by the You.

Kurt Lewin called them "We Feelings" such as cohesiveness, closeness, distance, overwhelmedness, estrangement, good or bad communications, high and low tensions, and so on. These all generate from "in-between" partners. It is to the regulation of these "in-between" qualities that the pairing system addresses itself.

The theoretical frame of reference for the pairing system is a mixture of personality theory (humanistic psychology orientation) and Lewinian field theory. The practical educational-therapeutic function of the pairing system is its utility in making man's ambitious quest for intimacy less mystifying and more attainable. This is attempted by offering contact-making communication styles that facilitate dealing with conflicts and tensions. In this conception the pairing system explicitly assumes that aggression can be trained into the service of love and intimacy (Ref.: Bach and Wyden).

These basic hypotheses are research-testable. Some relevant research projects are in progress, some are completed (e.g. Selection of Intimacy-Potentials; Longitudinal Stages in the Development of Familiarity). Obviously, the urgent task in future research is to pinpoint variables that further the development of intimacy, and differentiate them from those that hinder such development. A long and difficult program of research is before us, but it is one that should be undertaken, especially by objective researchers not as deeply involved in clinical work as we are.

CAN YOU TEACH INTIMACY?

The quest for intimacy being a fact, who is going to guide it? With Margaret Mead, we believe that professional psychologists should not promote new standards for living that most people cannot reach. According to Eric Berne, only a small psychological elite can be expected to understand true intimacy, let alone live it.

We hold that people do not *have* to play anti-intimate games. Such games can be eliminated in favor of exercises that train them to reach out, touch others, open up, and give of themselves. These exercises ae not manipulative tricks. They are new ways of relating to people. These new ways are best and most clearly learned as behavior and communication styles, demonstrated by methods that are emerging from encounter group experiences. Such new behavior styles can be programmed and taught through simple practice, even outside the growth groups. This educational, rather than manipulative, spirit is the guiding idea for the various interaction exercises reported in this book. There is, of course, always the danger that some students (and unfortunately some trainers, too) might misuse these new behavior patterns as manipulative tactics and strategies. Every movement has its opportunists—but we can teach people how to recognize them and protect themselves from them.

THE TRAINING OF PAIRING COACHES

Except for Dr. Bach, the innovator of the pairing system, a pairing coach in our program must be single, i.e. never married or widowed or divorced. This qualification is demanded by the principle of learning from the model. Also, through identification with his students, the single coach is as free as possible of any feeling of being different from them.

Another qualification for the pairing coach is a broad education in comparative cultures. This will hopefully free the coach of chauvinism concerning such stereotyping as femininity and masculinity. In accepting people for training as pairing coaches, we believe that an academic specialization in one or more of the following fields may facilitate eventual competence: group dynamics, clinical psychology, applied sociology, psychodrama, group therapy, sensitivity training, marriage and family counselling, sexology, social work, semantics, and the dramatic verbal and nonverbal arts. Ideally, a pairing coach is at home in several of these fields.

Background, while necessary for initial selection of training candidates, carries, of course, less weight than what the training candidate actually will do, how effective he will be in teaching pairing to adult singles, how well his trainees learn to enrich the meaning and the joy of the single existence.

The training of professional pairing coaches starts with their own participation in the program that they are eventually to teach their students.

Notes on Chapter 3

THE "PAIRING VILLAGE"

The term "pairing village" is a poetic adaptation of the more sober conceptual notion by Karl Marx of the social *nexus*, adopted by Sartre and more recently by Laing. Kurt Lewin's concept of "life space" is another conceptualization as are J. L. Moreno's subjective sociograms. The psychological basis for all these related concepts is the basic insight into the interdependent nature of the individual, who, for growth and survival, requires more or less constant resonating interaction with emotionally, intellectually, and economically relevant and thereby significant others.

Notes on Chapter 4

"MATCHING"

Pointing out that the computer match-making business plies its trade in theoretical darkness does not mean that there is no light on the whole subject. On the contrary: one of the most vigorously pursued current objectives of psychological research is to pinpoint the variables that affect the vicissitudes of interpersonal attraction. Compared to crude pseudotheorizing in terms of similarities, "opposites," reference-group memberships, and so on, the problems studied are sophisticated, focusing for example on complex relationships between attraction and the following variables: the congruity or dissonance of self-esteem and regard by others; the conditions under which perceived preference will or will not be reciprocated by liking; the effects of ingratiation (accommodation and collusion) on the development of intimacy. A good example of theoretical and methodological sophistication characteristic of scientific research in this area are the studies on intersexual attraction by Ellen Berscheid and Elain Walster (see Bibliography).

Notes on Chapter 5

"PLEASE TOUCH"

Jane Howard's autobiographical guided tour through the various centers of the human potential movement, as contained in her book *Please Touch*, is significant reportage. Her remarkable odyssey through dozens of marathon experiences started with Dr. Bach. (Ref.: Jane Howard's chapter, *"Transparency at Midnight,"* in which one of the pairing weekends for adult singles conducted by our institute at Kairos, is described in vivid, autobiographical color.)

"THINGING"

The "thinging" concept was originally developed by us as an explanatory principle to account for the radical change of state from peaceful affection to violent homicide. Seventy-three spouse-killers were interviewed in prisons in six countries on three continents. The findings, as yet unpublished, suggest that a cognitive metamorphosis that changes a human person into an inhuman "thing" is a necessary (although not sufficient) cognitive condition for killing a spouse. The ethical significance of this finding is that the human species, contrary to Konrad Lorenz's pessimistic denial, does have a strong inhibitor to genocide: the human victim must first be transformed into a "thing" before deliberate killing of that thing can take place. Prevention, therefore, would logically indicate the avoidance of symbolization, the vigorous pursuit of identity-facilitating humanization of all strangers, reduction of in-group love and out-group hate, counteracting political "pseudospecification," and vigorously exposing the tendency to depersonalize people in times of stress.

ROLE REVERSAL

The concept and technique of role reversal has been adapted to pairing training from its origins in psychodramatic and sociodramatic procedures given to us by the pioneer, J. L. Moreno.

NONLINGUISTIC GESTURES

Nonlinguistic gestures are another expression of the urgent quest for authentic contact in a culture dominated by verbal media. Dr. David Wessel collaborated with Dr. Bach while at Michigan State

University to compose a "symphony of intimately aggressive vocal gestures." The original performance involving a chorus of over three hundred vocalizers occurred in May 1970 on the East Lansing campus. The composition contains a combination of the elements of the pairing system and the so-called "foeing" system (Ref.: Bach, 1970). Pairing training includes an understanding of the transmitting functions of accessibility and rejection signals of body postures and vocal gestures. The most sophisticated research in this area is being conducted by Professor Birdwhistell and his associates at the University of Pennsylvania. The presentation in this volume of the contrast between open-receptive and closed-exclusive pairing stances represents a beginning of the application of a growing field of knowledge to the achievement of true intimacy.

MEDITATION

The utility of meditation is the transcendence of situationally induced anxiety. A crude parallel could be drawn with the desensitization exercises developed by Dr. Wolpe and other behavior-modifying therapists. Meditation produces a relatively more relaxed state conducive to gaining a perspective on the various options for action available at choice points. The Hindu, Buddhist, and Zen perspectives on meditation are inspirational and derive their utility from the strengthening of autonomy. This, obviously, differs from our use of meditation in the service of interpersonal realities. Practically speaking, our type of meditation seeks to make action options more explicit to the meditator, so that he may know more clearly what he wants and how to convey his wishes to his partner.

HUDDLING WITH THE COACH

The consulting services of a professional pairing coach include, but are not restricted to, the teaching and supervision of practicing behavior patterns that maximize openness and communication. An additional function of the pairing coach is to assist the potential pairer to become clear as to what he really wants and what he does not want in a given pairing. All possible options are reviewed by the coach in a verbal conference called the "huddle." Many of the comments by the coaches contained in the text of this book can be recognized as helping to display options of approach.

Notes on Chapter 10

REJECTION WITHOUT FEAR

Since rejection and exploitation are two basic fears of single adults, the pairing system uses exercises to reduce these fears. The act of rejecting someone also instigates negative tensions, such as the fear of counterrejection, and also guilt over "hurting" someone. Through the rejection exercises, trainees can enlarge their tolerance for rejection as well as reduce their qualms about rejecting. Partners will watch each other carefully to see how each takes rejection of his person, ideas, or sexuality. Will he or she take rejection like a mature adult or like a baby? Paradoxically, certain styles of rejection-absorption are attractive, capable of reversing negative initial attitudes. Consequently, our training teaches how to reject constructively with a minimum of hurt. The overcoming of rejection stimulates involvement. A secondary aim is to prevent singles from using rejection fears to avoid the rejection risks of reaching out. Our training also includes the acting out of rejection-fear fantasies, thus subjecting illusionary fears of rejection to the type of reality testing practiced in reality therapy (Ref.: Glasser).

Notes on Chapter 11

TWO TYPES OF AGGRESSION

The distinction between hostility-type aggression and impact-type aggression is crucial. Hostility aggression is basically controlled by channeling it through rituals such as the male/female gender club, in which the sexes use as weapons an endless variety of stereotypical put-downs. After such ritualized hostilities are repeatedly experienced, they tend to disappear from intimate communication. Then aggression can have constructive impact.

Notes on Chapter 12

POLARIZATION

Polarization, conflict, and aggression. These core-notions of the pairing system find scientific validation in the tension-and-conflict theories developed by Kurt Lewin and the related theories of striving for "balance" by Heider, and concern with "dissonance" by Festinger. Ethologists, such as Konrad Lorenz, also have theoretically stressed, as well as observationally pointed to, the energizing value of conflict and aggression in the pairing behavior of some animal species other than man.

The attraction inherent in polarity is probably the challenge of resolving conflicting differences and/or the competitive stimulation of gauging oneself against a stranger. Polarity serves as an effective antidote to narcissistic conceit. It helps to delineate individuality through the differentiation of opposites. The pairing system promotes the open expression of polarities—as between members of different cultures—in order to overcome fears of the unfamiliar or unknown. Each partner must be clear about his own position, so that the other can differentiate himself. Thus the identity of each is clarified. Polarity also increases tolerances for differences, facilitates making allowances, and granting handicaps, as in the intimate relationship between the mother and her infant.

Our basic thesis is that vital pairing derives from the tensions created by polarities. The major joy of pairing occurs when two lovers are involved in maintaining a creative balance (not a poor third-best compromise) between the opposing forces inherent in intimate interdependence. Too much polarization between what he wants, is, or does and what she wants, is, does, feels, thinks, expects, represents unbearable imbalances or dissonances. Good polarized pairing is, however, never dull, because there is always some struggle as to which side of the polarity shall prevail. There will be frequent changes, as sometimes this pole and at other times the opposite pole dominates. The best clinical symptom or sign that pairing has lost its polar tensions is boredom. Boredom occurs when each partner supplies every wish and whim to the other without a struggle. The most basic polarity is sex ("Will she or won't she?") This is why instant sex, giving or taking immediate sensuous satisfaction without a struggle, without resistances to overcome, brings pleasure momentarily—but is boring in the longer run. Pairers will respect the power of resistance—including the "*no*"—and the power of surrender.

SEX DIFFERENCES

Today many people are questioning the validity of dramatizing so-called sex differences. Our own clinical experience and research suggest that people who like to maximize the obvious biological differences between males and females also tend to struggle with their own identities and see themselves as belonging to a well-defined sex-role class. The stereotyping of sex roles in advertising and in the entertainment media probably is largely responsible for the widespread exaggeration of sex differences. From the point of view of pairing, this overemphasis renders the meaningful relating of the sexes more conflictful than it needs to be. In this light, the influence on our culture of the Women's Liberation Movement (*sans* its counterphobic anti-masculinity) may yet have a progressive influence in promoting a concept of the whole human being.

Notes on Chapter 14

THE VALUE OF CONFLICT

The notion that conflict is inherent in interdependence is self-evidently true. But since conflict tends to be painful, it is always subject to denial and evasion in the traditional courting system. In contrast, pairing training not only teaches the acceptance of the reality of conflict but also the utilization of conflict to increase the joys of interdependence through the mastery of conflicts. That conflicts can be either defeatingly depressive and/or joyfully inspirational is evidenced by competitive sports. Our conflict-oriented pairing rests on the basic assumption that healthy men and women, far from being conflictphobic, seek conflicts in order to master them. Working out conflicts together creates involvement and commitment.

LEVELING

The concept of leveling was first advanced by the late Dr. Fred Stoller. Leveling is a model style of interaction in marathon encounter groups (see Glossary). The first marathon group was co-conducted by George Bach and Fred Stoller in the fall of 1963 in Palm Springs, California.

MOLDING

A semantically popular differentiation is made in psychotherapy and psychiatry between verbal and nonverbal methods. We agree with Birdwhistell that "nonverbal" is a misnomer. We prefer to differentiate in terms of body-expressive, verbal—expressive, vocal-expressive, hand-expressive, and the like.

Molding is an adult expression of doll-play, the adult equivalent of a young child's relationships with the world through clay and/or dolls. (See Bach's research on doll play in Bibliography.)

The pairing system at times promotes *therapeutic* regressions to childlike playfulness. The adult acting out of what the transactional theory of Eric Berne (See Bibliography) describes as "the child" can confer strong valency. Molding is one of several of the pairing exercises that promotes such creative regression. "Greaseball" and the "Bacata-beating" games are examples of allowing adults to play-act like aggressive-competitive children.

In addition to providing cue values for the release of ordinarily controlled childlike experiences, molding provides artistic expressions. Also, the quiet, verbally nonfluid person will find enormous release in the transverbal forms of expression.

Allowing oneself passively to be molded facilitates a most unusual experience of total trust, surrender, and renunciation of self-direction as one submits to the designer.

Notes on Chapter 16

PLAYFUL MOCK BEATINGS

The Bacata exercise finds its parallel in erotic beating fantasies that have been carefully investigated by psychoanalytically oriented researchers. We are currently engaged in a study that aims to specify the necessary and sufficient conditions under which playful mock beatings, either given or received, tend to enhance and/or retard sexual satisfactions.

Notes on Chapter 17

CONTRACTUAL RELATIONSHIPS

The as-if relationship suggests that contract arrangements are deterrents to intimacy. This is generally true, but even in ideal intimacy some contracts must be negotiated and honored, e.g. the setting of broad limits of tolerance, and the definition and respect of beltlines below which blows are intolerable. The psychology of contractual relationships is receiving a great deal of attention by researchers. Hopefully, contractual arrangements will lose some of their cultural prestige, but at present contracts usually provide easy devices for sexual and other exploitations.

PROS AND CONS OF AFFAIRS

The most cogent paper on the pros and cons of extramarital affairs is by the veteran psychiatrist Dr. Spurgeon English, who has contrasted its bad social reputation with its intrinsic values.

SET-UP OPERATIONS

We first observed set-up operations in group psychotherapy (Bach, "Intensive Group Psychotherapy," 1954). It was noticed that group members presented themselves as a certain image (sex object, mother figure, wise old man, baby, etc.) and then drew image-validating responses from others. Set-up operations are intuitive and operate by positively reinforcing image-validating reactions while ignoring or minimizing image-denying reactions.

Notes on Chapter 18

THE IRRELEVANCE OF RECIPROCITY AND PARITY IN GENUINE INTIMACY

One of the criteria of authentic pairing is the giftlike giving of that part of self that is, in receiving, experienced by the partner as a *unique* contribution. Such contributions are in amount and quality characteristic of the giver: his or her thing, his way of "impacting," stimulating, influencing the other. Such intimate giving cannot be matched, or "reciprocated" in equal kind or equal value (parity). Consequently, pairing does not have a balanced accounting system. On the contrary, the mark of true intimacy is more likely disparity, off-balance, and unilateral giving or taking. True intimacy is the opposite of a sound economic or judicial system in ordinary human cooperative dealings between (non-intimate) people. In well-functioning pairs, the partners develop a high tolerance (even enjoyment) of disparities, while those who tend to insist on achieving reciprocity end up with a reliable but dull, role-bound, contractually orderly system. One of the joys (and sorrows) of intimate pairing is precisely the freedom from contracts that insure parities. What really counts in intimacy are the *effects* that any of the unique contributions have on the partnership. This is very pair-specific. In many of the deepest pairings we have observed that one partner continually takes from the other something he could never repay in any way. Only if ever the genuine wants and needs of intimate partners were basically the same, would the quest for reciprocity and parity make any sense at all.

The traditional courtship pattern of seeking similarity (rather than stimulating polarity) felt "right" because "similars" do not need to develop a high tolerance for unique differences. Private-intimate systems developed by "similars" conform more smoothly with the expectations of reciprocity and parity prevailing in ordinary social, cooperative—but not deeply intimate—relationships. Synthetic contractual bonds are always in danger of breaking over conflicts as to who takes more and who gives more. Fighting over reciprocity and parity are symptoms of contractual-exploitive relationships, not of genuine pairing relationships.

Notes on Chapter 19

DISCONTINUOUS PAIRING

Discontinuity, which is typical in the pairing of singles, has the obvious advantage of greater individual freedom over continuous contact pairing—such as in marital and nonmarital living together. However, discontinuity also creates tensions because partings as well as re-entries are anxiety evoking. If the stark realities of discontinuity—the yo-yo-like in and outness of such intimacy—are mismanaged or the problems inherent in disruption and re-entry are ignored or denied (by focusing exclusively on the "sweetness of the lovers' parting sorrow (as recommended by Shakespeare), then discontinuity will alienate and eventually destroy pairing.

Apartness invites projective fantasies. As on a Rorschach ink-blot test card, pairers apart have strong tendencies to dream, daydream, and to "think" about the absent other: what he may be doing, thinking, feeling. From such *imaging* tends to emerge a highly distorted mind-picture of the absent person. For partners with high levels of self-esteem the fantasies of the "state of the union," are positive and rosy mind-pictures. For those who are insecure about their own self-value the outlook is bleak; alienation or paranoid-suspicion of "disloyalty" are the themes. In both cases the mind pictures lead to type-casting and eventually to "thinging." As the time of the reunion of the pairers approaches, the imaging—if indulged in without restraints—will have produced definite expectations of how wonderfully loving and/or awfully rejecting the coming together will be. Since such expectations were developed by unilateral unchecked "clairvoyant' imaging, they are totally unrealistic and subject to frustrations and disappointments for certain. This will make the re-entry at the return tense and anxious instead of joyful. Worse, such expectations are stubborn. As with all other forms of unilateral narcissistic fantasies, partners try hard to make them come true, which leads to the further complication of engaging in manipulative "set-up operations," i.e. trying to maneuver the returning partner into behavior patterns congruent with the actually unrealistic expectations, and becoming really angry when the returning partner resists complying.

THEORY OF PARTING

Rasch and other psychiatrically oriented crimonologists have advanced a "parting" theory of homocide: the motive for killing a loved person is an inability to tolerate being left by him or her (Ref.: Bach and Hurley). These are extreme examples of the normal separation anxiety felt by all pairers.

Acknowledgments

THE good will and remarkable skills of a number of people were indispensable to the writing of this book. Catherine Mary Bond was instrumental in the development of the pairing system from its inception and remains an active teacher-practitioner. Yetta Magarick Bernhard, Co-Director of the Institute of Group Therapy, contributed valuable observations, ideas, and practical methods together with our group of trainers: Bronwyn Emery, Ruthe Gluckson, Dr. Lee Myerhoff, Dr. A. W. Pearson, Alex Vilumsons. Roger Bach, at the University of Utah, has designed research methods to validate and refine the pairing system, with a focus on rejection dynamics.

In reacting with constructive criticisms on their own pairing experiences, Claudia and Stephanie Bach have provided valuable validations.

The members of our pairing classes, in their candid group discussions, provided the basic data for this book. Particularly instructive were the participants in the marathon-type weekend meetings, and many individuals gave generously of their time in follow-up interviews.

Maria Wright also assisted creatively in the work and particularly contributed to our rejection research. Beatrice Tyler was of crucial assistance in many ways, including the preparation of the bibliography. Lynne Coren, Joan Hotchkiss, Meredith Mac-Rae, Pamela Pratt helped to demonstrate and to refine communication exercises and also served as participating resource persons in our research. David Hayes and Donald P. Estavan were the research consultants on the "computer dating" experiment. Lewis D. Hart designed and executed the research on first impressions. Bob Driver and his staff at the Kairos Human Growth Center on several occasons provided the climate for objective exploration of problems of single adults. Harry Marx aided in the use of videotape feedback technique in pairing practice sessions. Dr. John Hurley facilitated our teaching and research on pairing on the campus of Michigan State University in the spring quarter of 1970. Edwin C. Monsson helped design and organize adult education programs on pairing techniques at the University of California at Los Angeles. As the Institute's office manager, Johanna Vilumsons, aided by Barbara Searcy, planned and coordinated most effectively the seemingly endless meetings, recordings, and documents of our group and individual programs.

Peter Wyden, our publisher-editor, provided valuable and detailed suggestions as to the structure and format of this presentation.

Finally, we are most grateful to Peggy Jane Bach for creating a setting in her home in which the authors themselves could practice creative aggression to arrive at the authentic synthesis of a true collaboration.

G. R. B.
R. M. D.

Index

315